BRAVE BOYS CAN CHANGE THE WORLD

MATT KOCEICH

BRAVE BOYS CAN CHANGE THE WORLD

DEVOTIONS & PRAYERS FOR MAKING A DIFFERENCE

BARBOUR **kidz**
A Division of Barbour Publishing

Published by Barbour Publishing, Inc., 1810 Barbour Drive, Uhrichsville, Ohio 44683, www.barbourbooks.com

Our mission is to inspire the world with the life-changing message of the Bible.

Member of the
Evangelical Christian
Publishers Association

Printed in China.

001486 0223 DS

BRAVE BOY, *YOU* CAN CHANGE THE WORLD!

Let no one show little respect for you because you are young.
Show other Christians how to live by your life. They should
be able to follow you in the way you talk and in what you do.
Show them how to live in faith and in love and in holy living.

1 TIMOTHY 4:12

With each turn of the page, you'll discover that even though you're young, you can make a difference in the world. Each devotional reading will encourage you to embrace God's plan for your life, use your God-given gifts and abilities, and share the Good News in your neighborhood, community, and beyond. You'll be challenged to make a positive change in the world around you as you rely on the heavenly Father for courage and strength. Every page of this devotional offers a new adventure as you get started on your way to becoming a brave world changer!

WORLD CHANGER

*The Good News came to you the same as it is now going
out to all the world. Lives are being changed, just as your
life was changed the day you heard the Good News.*

COLOSSIANS 1:6

You're a special boy, and you're deeply loved by the Lord Jesus. He wants to use you to do mighty things in the world. You were created with a combination of very specific God-given gifts and talents that no one else has! Think about all the things you like to do and begin to consider how you might use those talents to change the world for Jesus.

All journeys start with the first step. As you think about how God wants to use you to change your world, remember that His plans are always best. Read His Word and connect your days—whether at home or school—to the things that matter to Him.

To take your first step on this brand-new, world-changing journey with Jesus, say a prayer. Tell Jesus everything. He loves you *so* much! Listen to His heart leading you through your Bible. Get ready to be amazed at how much God is going to do through your life.

*Dear Lord, thank You for the chance to be a part of Your great
adventure. I can't wait to see where Your path will lead me. Help
me to be brave as I set out to tell the world about You!*

BECAUSE OF JESUS

"If anyone wants to keep his own life safe, he will lose it. If anyone gives up his life because of Me and because of the Good News, he will save it."

MARK 8:35

It's hard not to be selfish. It's so easy to want things and collect stuff. We like to think about ourselves most of the time, but Jesus is calling you on a greater adventure to change your world.

God has given us so many good examples in His Word—true stories of people giving up their lives to share the gospel. In particular, the apostle Paul traveled all around the world telling anyone who would listen how much Jesus loved them. He wasn't ashamed to preach that Jesus died for their sins and was the one and only Savior.

Take some time today to think about your own journey to tell the world about Jesus. Where will it begin? In your home? Your school? Your neighborhood? Ask the Lord to put a person in your path whom you will be able to point to Jesus. It's so exciting to know that God is planning big things for your life!

Lord, help me not to be selfish. Help me to want what You want. Help me change my life so all of my choices will help others know how much You love them. Thank You, Jesus!

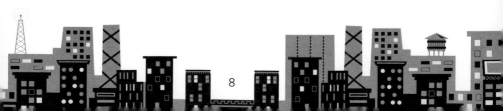

MAKE HIM FAMOUS

*"I tell you, everyone who makes Me known to men, the Son
of Man will make him known to the angels of God."*
Luke 12:8

Can you imagine? . . . Jesus says that when you make Him known to others,
He makes you known to the angels in heaven! It's amazing to know that
when you spend your time telling your friends about Jesus, He tells the
angels about you! So dream big. Start thinking about how you can reach
many people for His glory.

When you think about famous people, it's easy to see how everyone
knows about them. Maybe they're sports stars or popular actors. Maybe
they're on TV or they're bestselling authors. Whatever path brought them
fame, one thing is sure: everyone knows them because people talk about
them.

One way to help make Jesus famous is by sharing all the lessons He
teaches you in life. Keeping a journal is a great way to track the lessons He
is teaching you. Don't be overwhelmed about sharing Jesus with others.
It will never be you versus the world. It's *always* you and Jesus together,
wherever you go to make Him known.

*Jesus, people want to be around popular people. I really want
to make You more famous than the most famous person on
earth. Help me to be brave and promote Your mighty name!*

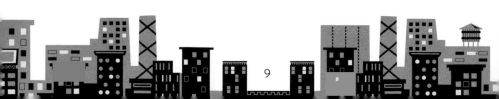

STRONG HOPE

*Our hope comes from God. May He fill you with joy
and peace because of your trust in Him. May your
hope grow stronger by the power of the Holy Spirit.*
ROMANS 15:13

So many things in this world are competing for your attention. You might feel really good about sharing your faith with a friend, but then something distracts you and you don't. On your new adventure to change the world for Jesus, you'll encounter a ton of speed bumps and detours. Some days you might wake up and just not feel good. Other times you might feel nervous. That's where God comes in!

He promises you that He will never leave your side. You are a team. That truth can help you when you think you're not smart enough or brave enough to share the good news with people.

Through His Spirit, God is always there to give you joy and direction for your life. Focus on His commands. Make good choices that will help you know your life is in line with His teachings. Think of one thing you can do today that will bring Him glory. He's proud of you!

*Lord, sometimes I get distracted from what You want me to do,
and I forget You're in charge. Please help me to remember
to put my hope only in You. Help me always to trust
You. Please fill my heart with Your peace.*

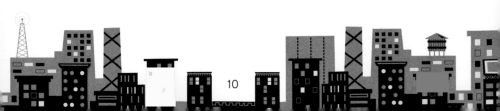

REAL LOVE

We have come to know and believe
the love God has for us. God is love.
1 John 4:16

Jesus says you are very, very special! He made you with unique gifts and personality traits and spends every moment of your life loving you. And He wants you to know how real His love is. Like the sun that warms you on a chilly morning or the brilliant stars that light up a dark night sky, the real love of Jesus is always there to bring you comfort and peace.

His "for real" love for you never ends! It fills every inch of your heart and constantly reminds you that no matter what, Jesus holds you close. He wouldn't have it any other way.

Feel His arms embrace you and give you strength.

Listen to His voice say you mean the world to Him!

There aren't enough words to describe how precious you are to Jesus. The Bible says His love for you is more than the endless grains of sand (Psalm 139:17–18)! Jesus loves you infinitely and unconditionally. Know you are loved by the Lord of lords and King of kings and that you are held safe in His loving arms. . .*forever.*

Thank You for loving me, Jesus! I can't make it through a
single day without Your love. Please show me how to be more
like You—how to love more like You—every single day.

ON HIGH PLACES

The Lord God is my strength. He has made my feet like the feet of a deer, and He makes me walk on high places.

HABAKKUK 3:19

Deer are amazing animals. They can leap up the sides of rocky cliffs and get to places that people would have a very hard time reaching. A beautiful example of God's creativity, deer are graceful and able to run swiftly, as though they are flying.

The Old Testament prophet Habakkuk reminds us that God should always be the source of our strength. In this way you can become like a deer and go places you wouldn't normally be able to go and do things you wouldn't normally be able to do.

As you think about your world-changing journey, remember the Lord is your guide. Ask Him to lead you to the "high places" in your life. It could be a person, like a friend from school or church who may not have a personal relationship with Jesus. The "high place" might be for yourself, like this quiet time where you learn more about the Lord and His Word. Wherever or whatever it is, trust that God will give you all you need to get there!

Dear Lord, thank You for giving me a purpose. I really want to be brave and tell people about Your love and offer of forgiveness. Please give me the wisdom and strength to get to the high places in life.

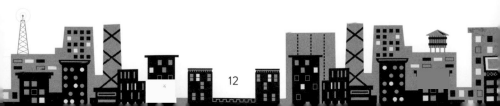

HE HEARS YOU

And it will be before they call, I will answer.
While they are still speaking, I will hear.
ISAIAH 65:24

Isn't it amazing to know that the God of the universe listens to you? Even before you call out to Him, He listens! Make talking to Him a daily habit—talk to him whenever and wherever you want! He *never* gets tired of hearing your voice. He wants to know everything you're feeling and everything you dream of.

The Bible is full of people who talked with God. Noah built the ark because he talked to God and was faithful. The woman at the well was fortunate enough to talk with Jesus face-to-face. He filled her heart so much that she couldn't help but run back to her village and tell everyone about Him. Many people believed in Jesus because of the woman's testimony.

What is on your heart that you can share with the Lord today? Is something stressful going on? Is there a problem you can't quite solve? Or maybe there's a person you're close to who doesn't know Jesus. Ask God for direction. He will never let you down.

Thank You, Lord, for listening to me. I need You. I need to know
You care. Please hear me. I'm working on sharing my faith
with my family and friends, but I can't do it without You.

ALL THINGS

I can do all things because Christ gives me the strength.
PHILIPPIANS 4:13

That's right—with Jesus, you have the ability to do some super amazing things. Whether you are outgoing or shy, you will be able to achieve so much more than you've ever imagined. Know that He is there to help you. You'll be grinning from ear to ear when you see all the ways Jesus will show up to help you through even the most difficult situations.

There are so many examples in your Bible where ordinary people did extraordinary things through the strength of Jesus. One great example is Jonah. He didn't want to go where God told him to go, but he eventually went to Nineveh and preached the message of the Lord. People's lives were changed because of Jonah's obedience.

What can you do that will lead others to the heart of Jesus?

Give all your time and energy to making Jesus famous in your little part of the world. Something as small as a kind deed for someone can help others see Jesus. You don't have to do anything super big, and it doesn't have to cost money. Planting seeds of hope in a friend's heart will not only let them know you care but also open a door for you to talk about Jesus down the road. God is so proud of you!

Lord, I believe You can help me do anything for Your glory. Please guide my steps as I think about sharing the gospel with others. Show me where to go and then give me strength to obey.

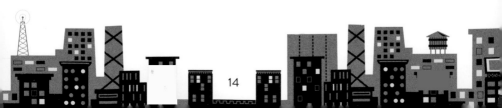

FOREVER

Our Lord Jesus Christ and God our Father loves us. Through His loving-favor He gives us comfort and hope that lasts forever.

2 THESSALONIANS 2:16

God has great plans for you, brave boy! Even before you were born, the Lord thought about you and came up with amazing plans for your life. He is always there to encourage you and help you live for Jesus.

Think about all the things God has given you—talents and abilities—and how you might be able to use them to share your faith with the people who live in your neighborhood. For example, if your family goes on walks, you could say a prayer as you walk past your neighbors' homes.

Jesus made a habit of loving ordinary people so much that they couldn't help but go and tell everyone about Him. Jesus' disciples weren't super-heroes, but they knew that Jesus believed in them and was always with them and ready to help. That was enough to move them to travel great distances and boldly tell others about their wonderful Savior. Are you ready to do the same?

Lord, to be honest, I've never really thought about sharing the gospel in big ways. I'll tell people that You are awesome, but I haven't given much thought to telling people that You died for their sins and want to have a personal relationship with them. Show me how to get started!

BREAD OF LIFE

Jesus said to them, "I am the Bread of Life. He who comes to Me will never be hungry. He who puts his trust in Me will never be thirsty."

<small>JOHN 6:35</small>

Jesus is your teacher. When He said that one of His names is "Bread of Life," He was telling people that He is their *everything*. As you grow, remember that Jesus knows what's best for you. Let Him lead you through your Bible. Read His words and keep a journal of the lessons He teaches you. You'll be surprised at how many new things you learn!

The world we live in has so many distractions. It's hard to focus on living for Jesus if we're constantly thinking about ourselves or all the stuff we want. Having a humble heart means you're willing to do things the way God wants you to do them, even when it seems hard. Thinking about Jesus helps you make good choices as you follow Him.

Sharing your faith is one of those good choices. It's a big step, but you can do it! Telling people that Jesus will be with them, no matter what, helps them know about His love. Jesus is their answer! Jesus is *the* answer!

Lord, thank You for saving me and always taking care of me. Thank You for meeting all my needs. Help me get back on track when I lose focus. Help me to remember all the lessons You're teaching me so I can remind everyone I know that You are the Bread of Life.

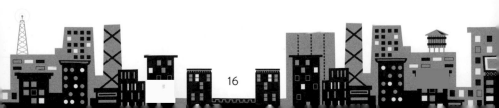

NOT ASHAMED

Hope never makes us ashamed because the love of God has come into our hearts through the Holy Spirit Who was given to us.
ROMANS 5:5

Jesus brought hope to the world in many ways. Out of love, He reached out to many different people. It didn't matter to Him if they were young or old, healthy or sick, rich or poor. Jesus listened. Jesus spoke words of healing. Jesus looked His friends in the eyes and let them know they mattered to Him.

God is calling you to treat people the same way Jesus did. It might seem scary at first, but He has given you the tools and opportunities you need to change the world in big ways. You might have doubts, but don't let those concerns keep you from boldly sharing the love of Jesus with your friends, family, and neighbors.

Take some time to think creatively. How can you begin to take Jesus' message of hope into your world? To the sick and brokenhearted, what words can you speak that will lead them to Jesus? One way you could offer hope is to make a card for someone who needs to be reminded that Jesus loves them. Or maybe you could help make a meal for someone who isn't feeling well. Building relationships is the first step on your world-changing journey!

Jesus, I'm grateful You keep loving me no matter what.
Please show me ways I can share Your love with others who
need to hear about it. Jesus, keep growing my hope in You.

PRAISE HIM!

*But the Lord favors those who fear Him and
those who wait for His loving-kindness.*
PSALM 147:11

You're not alone on your journey! The Lord is with you right now—and He always will be. That's good news! As you think of ways to share your faith, don't forget to praise Jesus along the way. After all, when you worship Him because of who He is, He'll favor you—He'll rain down blessings on you.

He is your shield and is always there to protect you. He is your safe place. He listens to you every time you talk to Him. The Lord is always finding ways to show you His love. He thinks you're pretty wonderful!

As you begin your world-changing journey, ask the Lord to open doors of opportunity for you. Remember, you praise Him when you make the right choices for your life, so choose well—even when no one else around you is doing the right thing. Jesus sees you and He's so proud!

God, it's amazing to think about everything You do for me. Help me to be content with what You've given me. I want to spend my days praising You for who You are and for all the blessings You give me.

WAITING FOR YOU

The Lord is not slow about keeping His promise as some people think. He is waiting for you. The Lord does not want any person to be punished forever. He wants all people to be sorry for their sins and turn from them.

2 PETER 3:9

This is a key verse for you to keep in mind as you plan your world-changing journey. The Lord is using you to be His hands and feet in the world, to go and tell people that He wants to forgive them of their sins. The loving Savior, Jesus, longs for the day when all His children repent and go running into His waiting arms.

Jesus promises to make a way for you to become brave and bold. He has many lessons for you—lessons to help you figure out how to use your talents for His good purposes. One of those lessons, found in the book of Matthew in your Bible, teaches the importance of being a peacemaker (see Matthew 5:9). When you're a peacemaker, you are showing others the love of Jesus. Speaking kind words to your family and friends is an easy way to practice spreading peace.

Think about how you felt when you first asked Jesus to forgive your sins and become your Savior. Use those feelings to fuel your passion to share Jesus with the world around you!

Please give me a heart for people who don't know You, Lord. Show me the way to go so I can share Your love with as many people as possible. Whatever You ask me to do, Lord, I will do it!

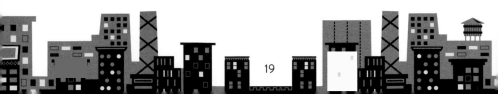

JOY

The Lord your God is with you, a Powerful One Who wins the battle. He will have much joy over you. With His love He will give you new life. He will have joy over you with loud singing.
ZEPHANIAH 3:17

Anytime you take a trip, there will be times when you need to take a break from the long car ride. That's why people stop at rest stops. Maybe you've gone to them with your family. Rest stops offer a chance to get a snack or two, grab some water, and stretch your legs.

On your new adventure of changing the world for Jesus, you will need to schedule spiritual rest stops. During these breaks, it's a great idea to read sections of your Bible, like the third chapter of Zephaniah and Psalm 139, so you can be reminded of just how much you matter to God. When you get tired or sad, it's easy to forget how much God is blessing you. Consider this list of truths:

- God knit you together in your mother's womb (Psalm 139:13).
- You are fearfully and wonderfully made (Psalm 139:14).
- The Lord your God is with you (Zephaniah 3:17).
- He will take great delight in you (Zephaniah 3:17).
- In His love He will no longer rebuke you (Zephaniah 3:17).
- He will rejoice over you with singing (Zephaniah 3:17).

Be encouraged and remember to live each day connected to all of God's promises. His joy over you is never-ending!

*Lord, thank You for always reminding me
that I matter. I praise Your holy name!*

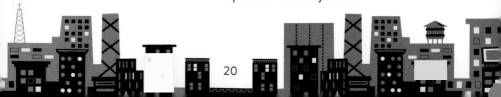

EVERYTHING

And my God will give you everything you need
because of His great riches in Christ Jesus.
PHILIPPIANS 4:19

Did you know that God will provide everything you need? Of course, that's not to say you won't have hard times—but it does mean the Lord promises to be there for you and help you through it all. In today's verse from Philippians 4, the apostle Paul told the church of believers in Philippi that they had great riches in Jesus.

As you work to share the gospel in your corner of the world, think about all the blessings you have because of Jesus. You are forgiven! Jesus sees you, not as a sum of your sins, but as His precious child whom He loves no matter what. You are a new creation! Jesus is transforming you to look and act more like Him each day.

Make a commitment to rely on God and all His promises for you. Pray daily and ask Him to guide you on the paths He wants you to take on your journey. He alone is the one who will open doors for you to share your story of how Jesus became your everything. This journey is so exciting! Be courageous for God's glory!

Thank You, Jesus, for always being there for me. Thank You for
being my biggest treasure. Keep me humble and help me to have
a thankful heart so that I never take Your blessings for granted.

NEVER EMPTY

*"So My Word which goes from My mouth will not return to Me empty.
It will do what I want it to do, and will carry out My plan well."*

Isaiah 55:11

When people travel, they make sure to pack the things they'll need. On your adventure to change the world, your Bible is the very best thing to have with you.

Scripture tells us that the Word of the Lord is God-breathed and sharper than a double-edged sword. When you read your Bible, you are planting God's words in your heart. Reading and thinking about His Word will begin to grow new knowledge within you so you can keep learning more and more about Him. When you make Bible reading a habit, your spiritual tank will always be full.

You know the Lord has big plans for your life. The more you stay in God's Word, the more you will begin to understand the pieces of His plan and how they all fit together. Keep praying and asking God to show you verses that highlight what is important to Him. Growing your faith by reading your Bible is a great way to make the most of your lifetime journey!

Lord, thank You for my Bible. Please help me to lean in and make reading it my top priority. Teach me how to live more like Jesus each day, and help me look for ways to tell others about His love.

HE IS FOR YOU

God is faithful.
1 CORINTHIANS 10:13

God is on your side. It makes sense if you think about it. . . . He created you with special talents and a wonderful heart. He loves you unconditionally and wants to see you succeed in everything you set out to do. His faithfulness will take you through each one of your days—He'll show you truth in His Word and gently guide you as you become more and more like Jesus.

Is there a person in your life who doesn't know Jesus? Pray and ask God to give you an opportunity to share your faith story. You will be surprised at how God blesses your willingness to get out of your comfort zone to tell people about His goodness.

Remember, God is *always* with you. He will never stop leading you to people who need to know they are loved. Let Him change your heart just a little each day so that you begin to want what He wants. Let God show you how faithful He is by trusting in His promise to keep you and never let you go.

Jesus, a lot of times I don't feel confident enough to talk to people about You. I don't want to upset anybody or make them think I'm not minding my own business. Please make a way for me to share Your love in a way that will be well received. Thank You!

ALL THE SAME

Men become right with God by
putting their trust in Jesus Christ.
ROMANS 3:22

Your world-changing journey is going to be epic! You are going to do so many amazing things for Jesus. And as you bring people the message of hope because of what Jesus did for them on the cross, you will find that your trust in Him becomes stronger, enabling you to make more courageous decisions. You might not like to talk in front of the class or a big group of kids, but the more you trust Jesus, the more you will feel confident to try doing things that you once thought were too scary.

Sometimes it's hard to remember that there was a time when you didn't know Jesus like you do today. The Bible says that everyone makes mistakes and needs Jesus. We're all the same. And when you recognize that's true, you will be able to see just how important your world-changing, Jesus-sharing mission really is.

You are special, and the Lord is calling you to be His brave and confident ambassador. He is ready to use you to share your faith with all who will listen. Jesus is proud of you!

Lord, it's hard to trust in things I can't see, but I know
in my heart You are here with me. I ask for boldness so that
I can tell people about Your saving grace. I want to shine
my light and lead my friends and family to You.

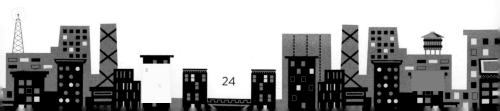

24

GIVE IT TO GOD

Give all your cares to the Lord and He will give you strength.
He will never let those who are right with Him be shaken.
PSALM 55:22

The Bible is filled with reminders of just how much God cares about you. He loves you and walks with you through every one of life's ups and downs. Some days you might feel sad or alone. Other days you might feel happy and full of energy. No matter how you feel, Jesus is always there to hold your hand. He's smiling and celebrating you when you're having good times, and He's there holding you close when you're going through hard times.

Jesus wants you to give Him all your worries and all the things that stress you out. He is bigger than all your bad days combined. The enemy, Satan, wants you to think that some situations are hopeless, but Jesus is your Savior who died for you so that you would always have hope!

God is faithful. He will always love you. He will never let you down. He will fight for you and give you everything you need. *Always.*

Jesus, thank You so much for caring about me and being with me
through every good time and every bad time. I am so grateful
for You. Help me to rely on You every moment of every day.
When I forget You're there, please forgive me. I love You, Lord.

BELIEVE

"Do not be afraid, just believe."
MARK 5:36

Jesus doesn't want you to live in fear of anything. He wants you to believe that He is big enough and loves you enough to take care of you. He gave His life for you. There's literally *nothing* He can't handle.

When you think about sharing Jesus with others, remember that He always wants what's best for you. Ask Him to show you times in His Word when He was faithful and took care of His children. The truth is He's with you *right now* doing the same. Trust Him. Believe that He loves you immeasurably and wants to lead you to the people and places that need to hear about His love and forgiveness.

Don't forget Jesus will never leave you alone. He is comfort and peace, hope and love, help and healing. Feel Him giving you all these blessings and more as you come to understand that with Him, you are right where you need to be. Let these truths fill every space of your heart, and then begin to map out your journey to change the world for Jesus!

Jesus, help me not to be afraid. Help me know You're here.
I believe! Lead me in Your ways forever. I will follow You.

REAL FAITH

Give all your worries to Him
because He cares for you.
1 PETER 5:7

Tell Jesus what's on your heart, and then ask Him to lead you today. Practice being silent before Him and listen for His voice. He will help you recall certain Bible verses or stories that will help you face the day.

Jesus cares for you—and that will never, ever change! Living your life to bring Him glory is the best use of your time. Think about ways you can share His love with others who need to know that He wants to take away their worries and cares too.

Your faith isn't like a magic trick. You don't have to say a certain number of prayers and then Jesus will magically grant your wishes like a spiritual genie. Putting your trust in the one who made you and loves you is what will establish the real relationship Jesus wants. Take time to think about how important you are to God—and then thank Him for saving you. Becoming the brave boy you were created to be will overflow your heart with joy!

Lord, my Savior, help me when I start to worry. Please teach me
how to be still and listen for Your quiet voice. Help me to give
You everything—especially those things that cause me to worry.

HIS LOVING-KINDNESS

*Honor and thanks be to God! He has not turned away from
my prayer or held His loving-kindness from me.*
PSALM 66:20

Let everything you do honor God. Think about how awesome He is, and be thankful for all the ways He blesses you and your family. God is always there to give you joy, even in the middle of your worst days. Take comfort in knowing that He wants to hear everything you say—always.

Jesus built relationships with people. He loved and served others through the words He spoke and the things He did. Jesus made sure His friends knew they were loved and cared for.

How might you spread God's loving-kindness in your home? In your school? In your community? Maybe you could help a sibling with homework or chores. Maybe you could organize a canned food drive to help people in need. Or maybe you could volunteer with your parents at church to be a blessing to a bigger group of people. Whatever you do, use the opportunities God gives to make Him famous!

*Jesus, thank You for always being with me. Please let me
feel Your loving-kindness so I can be a bigger blessing to
others. Thank You for loving me so perfectly, Lord.*

HIS GOODNESS

For You are good and ready to forgive, O Lord.
You are rich in loving-kindness to all who call to You.
PSALM 86:5

You mean the world to Jesus. He doesn't want you to feel shame when you make mistakes. He's there to forgive you when you ask. He's got your back 24-7.

The enemy, Satan, doesn't like your relationship with Jesus. He tries to keep you far away from the Lord. He'll put distractions in your path, hoping you'll spend your time on things that take you away from your world-changing adventure.

Stay connected to Jesus by making a daily habit of reading His Word. Studying your Bible will help you know what's important to God. Spend time thinking about what you learn, and find ways to practice those lessons at home and school. You may have days when you feel like you aren't sharing Jesus enough. Don't stress. The Lord knows your heart. He uses even the little things you do for His glory. He pours out His goodness over every part of your day so you will always be taken care of. You are dearly loved!

Lord, I'm so grateful You love me and think I'm special.
Please forgive me when I mess up. I don't want my
mistakes to keep me from telling people about You.
Thank You for always listening to me. I love You, Jesus.

HOLY CONFIDENCE

*For the Lord your God is the One Who
fights for you, just as He promised you.*
JOSHUA 23:10

God is a promise keeper. He loves you—and His feelings for you will never change. He wants you to be confident that He has the very best plans for your life. He sees you and knows what you're going through. Remember that you are never alone.

When you think about sharing the love of Jesus with the world, don't forget that you have the power of the Holy Spirit on your side. You will be strong and protected because the Bible says God is your shield.

Knowing these truths, think about this: In what area of your life do you need to trust God more? Are you worshipping Him throughout the week—or only on Sundays at church? Maybe you can listen to some praise songs during the week to help keep your mind on Him. Are you having a hard time reading your Bible? Start reading a little—and then add more as you go. The Gospel of Mark is a great place to start learning all about the majesty of Jesus.

Knowing that God is for you changes everything. Ask Him to lead you. Let Him love you. With the holy confidence that comes only from God, go tell your friends and family that He is the Savior and King.

*Jesus, please show me how to serve You and others better.
Give me confidence to tell people everything You have done
for me. Help me to want what You want more than anything else.*

HOPE

And now, Lord, what do I wait for? My hope is in You.
PSALM 39:7

Hope is when you want and expect a certain thing to happen. When you put your hope in God, you can trust that He is always for you. Waiting can be hard, but when you've put your hope in God's plan and timing, you never have to worry.

Many people in the Bible put their hope in the Lord but had to wait for His perfect timing. Moses was eighty years old when God sent him back to Egypt to help rescue the Israelites! Joseph was in jail for thirteen years for something he didn't do. David waited fifteen years before he could become king. Sarah waited twenty-five years to have her son, Isaac. And Rebekah waited twenty years before she had her children, Jacob and Esau. Our human nature wants everything *right now*, but God doesn't work that way.

If we use our times of waiting in the right way, we have the opportunity to grow our faith and our prayer life, and draw even closer to Jesus.

Lord, teach me how to wait. Remind me that You haven't left me alone even on days when it feels like I am. Help me lean into Your arms and Your love. Thank You for holding me and never letting go.

YOUR SAVIOR

But God showed His love to us. While we
were still sinners, Christ died for us.
ROMANS 5:8

Brave boy, do you know how important you are to Jesus? Not a day goes by when He isn't loving you and thinking about all the ways you are special to Him.

He doesn't just say these things in the Bible. He did something amazing to show you and everyone else how He feels about you. Jesus came to save you when there was no way you could save yourself. Your sins and mistakes and mess-ups made you like a stranger to God, but when Jesus took up His cross to pay the ultimate price through the ultimate sacrifice, everything changed. And when you asked Him to become your Savior, His love washed over you and connected your heart to His.

Let that same connection inspire you to share His great sacrifice with others. God will provide opportunities for you to make friendships that will turn into chances to share your faith journey. For His glory, go and tell the world how He has changed your life!

Thank You, Jesus! I won't ever fully understand what You've done for me, but I pray that my life reflects a thankful heart. Please give me chances to tell others what an awesome thing You've done for us.

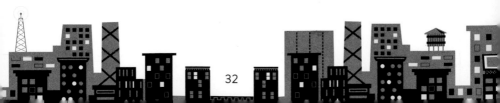

HIS TREASURE

You are of great worth in My eyes.
You are honored and I love you.
ISAIAH 43:4

You may not completely understand this. . .but you are God's treasure. Part of your world-changing adventure includes knowing who you are in Christ. Let His words be daily reminders that you matter and that your life has great purpose.

If you've ever experienced snow, then surely you've seen the sky turn gray and felt the temperature drop below freezing. Sometimes the sun stays hidden for days, but it eventually reappears—and when it does, the sky returns to blue, the temperature rises, and the snow begins to melt. This is a great picture of what happens in our lives when we feel disconnected from God. Those days are the snowy days of the soul—when the sun seems to have disappeared and our hearts hope for the warmth of our Savior.

This is when we need to be reminded that things will change. God will shine in your heart and melt away feelings of sadness and loneliness. Remember, just like the sun can be hidden behind dark clouds but still be present, Jesus is with you even on the hard days—even when you can't see Him. You are His precious child, and He loves you greatly.

Thank You for thinking so much of me, Lord. Help me feel the same way about myself. Sometimes I feel down and don't know how to make the negative feelings stop. I know the truth is that You love me and will never leave me. Help me know that You're enough.

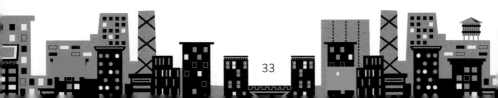

ANYTHING

Jesus looked at them and said, "This cannot be done by men but God can do anything."
MARK 10:27

God can do anything. He made the planets and galaxies, the stars and oceans, the plants and animals, and a billion other things. The coolest part is that out of everything He made, you are made in His image. He made you special and unique—there's only *one* you. Do your best to make the most of the wonderful life He has given you. Talk with Him every day. Love Him with all your might.

Connect with Jesus every day. That's what His disciples did, and their lives were better for it. They ate together, prayed together, shared life stories together, and helped others together. Jesus wants to hear what's on your heart. He wants you to give Him everything. Spending your days with Him is the best way to live your life. Reading your Bible and being quiet before Him will help you follow His best paths for you.

With God on your side, you can do anything. Not like bench-press an elephant, but more like change the world by spreading the good news that Jesus is the Savior!

Lord, thank You for creating me. Thank You for reminding me that You're on my side and that I can do so much more than I could ever imagine for Your kingdom and glory. Help me rely on You more and more each day!

GOOD WILL COME

So the Lord wants to show you kindness. He waits on high to have loving-pity on you. For the Lord is a God of what is right and fair. And good will come to all those who hope in Him.
ISAIAH 30:18

There will be days when you feel like you aren't making a difference. Don't let those difficult days bring you down. Jesus had bad days too! God will give you strength today to be courageous and step out in faith and share the love of Jesus.

Use the creativity the Lord has given you and think of ways you can be a blessing to others. When you receive kindness from God, it overflows and gives you a chance to pay it forward. Find ways to be a blessing even when it might be hard to see the reason God is asking you to help certain people. (God's plan may not always make sense to you.)

Remember that nothing you do for God is ever a waste. No prayer, no good deed, no act of kindness will ever go unnoticed by God. He is proud of you and will always take care of your needs. Follow Jesus and keep hoping in Him. He'll never let you down!

Thank You for all the ways You are good to me, Lord. I really can't even count them all. Help me remember all the blessings You give me. Thank You, Jesus, for being my Savior!

HE MAKES A WAY

God is my strong place. He has made my way safe.
2 Samuel 22:33

Is there something you worry about all the time? Maybe you're concerned about a particular friendship that has been hard because of a misunderstanding, or maybe you're worried about a subject in school that you can't quite figure out. . .and you wonder if things will ever get better.

When you make God your strong place, you are showing the world that He is most important to you. He is the one you rely on in good and bad times. He is the one who cares about you deeply. The Bible says that God is your refuge—he's the place you go to for protection from the storms. Stay close to Jesus all the days of your life, and you will *never* be alone.

Just as the sun always rises after the darkness of night, Jesus will always shine over you. His love will always be there to warm your heart. Jesus always makes a way for you, so set down your worries and grab His hand. Follow Him today and go where He leads. You will never have regrets, and your heart will always be filled.

Jesus, lead me away from stress and worry today. Take me to the place where Your love is needed most, and help me be brave enough to share it with someone who is worried or alone. Thank You for letting me be a part of Your world-changing plans!

FORGIVEN

*If we tell Him our sins, He is faithful and we can depend on Him to
forgive us of our sins. He will make our lives clean from all sin.*
1 JOHN 1:9

Everyone makes mistakes. As believers, we know that we can take our mess-
ups to Jesus and receive His cleansing forgiveness. Jesus doesn't want you
to keep anything inside. Share everything with Him. Ask Him to fill your
heart with His never-ending love and care.

We learn so much from reading the Bible. It's full of true stories about
people who made mistakes but then turned their lives around. One time at
a well Jesus met a woman who had made a lot of mistakes. Jesus forgave
her and saved her. She couldn't hold in her emotions, so she ran back to
her village and told anyone who would listen about the great love of Jesus.
Many people who heard her story put their faith in Jesus. Read her story
in John 4. The woman at the well is a great example of how the Lord can
turn our mistakes into opportunities to tell others about Him.

Make a habit of sharing your mistakes with Jesus and then telling Him
you're sorry. Feel His forgiveness wash over you. Walk in the light of His
love and take the message of His healing truth to your corner of the world
and beyond. God is proud of you, and He loves you very much.

*Thank You for forgiving me when I make mistakes, Lord. Please help me
trust You more and more so I can obey You all the time—not just when
it's easy. Guide me in Your truth and help me to be brave for Your glory.*

LOVED

God is love.
1 John 4:8

You are loved by God. And God doesn't just *say* He loves you. He *proved* it when He sent Jesus to take up the cross for you! Jesus was your loving sacrifice—He paid a debt you would never be able to pay on your own. Because of Jesus and your willingness to put your faith in Him, your salvation is complete, wrapped in the most beautiful love of all—the love of Christ.

The love that God has for you is unfailing. It will never let you down. His love brings comfort and peace. It fills your heart with hope and joy. It showers you with kindness and warms your soul on days when you feel cold and alone. God's love reminds you that you matter and that you mean everything to Him. His love is always stirring feelings of compassion in you.

Let the perfect love of Jesus be your anchor when the storms of life blow. Let His love motivate you to do good things for others. Let it guide you to people who need to hear a message of hope. Share His love and watch it change your world.

Thank You for loving me, Jesus. Thank You for going to the cross for my sins. I can't imagine what You went through for me and all people. Help me remember everything You've done for me so that if I'm ever feeling afraid or alone, I'll know how much You love me.

GOD KNOWS

*But as for me, I will watch for the Lord. I will wait
for the God Who saves me. My God will hear me.*

MICAH 7:7

There may be times when you feel like no one understands what you're going through. But God does! There may be times when you wish things in your life were different. God understands and He knows how you're feeling. There may be days or even weeks when nothing seems to be going right. Brave boy, God knows!

Not only does God know all these things, but He's right there with you making a way for you to experience His joy and peace. Have faith. Make God the reason for everything you do. It doesn't matter if no one knows when you do something nice, because God knows. The enemy wants you to believe that God doesn't really care about you. He wants you to doubt that you are loved eternally by the King.

Make a list of all the things that are causing you stress right now. Then take some quiet time and read each one of them to God. Let Him know how you feel. He promises to listen and really help you. You are His special child. He will help you live in peace.

*Lord, I am so thankful that You are always with me and that
You understand and care about everything I'm going through.
I need Your help, Jesus. Life seems so hard sometimes, and I
don't always know what to do. Show me how to do the right
thing even when it's hard and I feel like I can't do it on my own.*

ON YOUR SIDE

*"He has only man with him. But we have the Lord our
God with us, to help us and to fight our battles."*

2 Chronicles 32:8

Battles come in all shapes and sizes. There are the battles you see in movies where superheroes fight against villains. There are other battles you might have learned about in your history books at school. Bringing it to a personal level, you might feel like doing your homework is a battle of sorts. Or maybe there's a person you have a hard time getting along with, and it feels like a battle to you.

As you spend time with the Lord and read His Word, you will begin to understand that spiritual battles are taking place continually. The enemy doesn't like when God's children read their Bibles and pray, because that's when they learn how special they are. The devil wants people to feel alone and afraid. That's why Jesus says over and over for you not to be afraid but to just believe in Him.

Stay connected to Jesus. He promises to help you, no matter what you're going through. He loves you deeply and will always be on your side!

Thank You, Lord, for helping me. No matter how big or small my battle is, knowing that You are always with me brings comfort to my heart. Thank You for showing me how to face my struggles the best way—Your way.

EVERLASTING

The Lord came to us from far away, saying,
"I have loved you with a love that lasts forever. So I
have helped you come to Me with loving-kindness."
JEREMIAH 31:3

It's amazing to think that God loves you so much and that His love will never end! He is there with you, loving you, reminding you through His Word that you are precious to Him. What's important to you is important to Him. When you feel sad, He is there to comfort you. When you feel stressed about something, Jesus wants to take away your anxiety.

Each day you receive the gift of spending time with Jesus. To talk to Him. Listen for His voice. Study His words. Each day is also a chance for you to change your world one step at a time. Maybe it's through a kind word you speak to a friend or a good deed you do for a neighbor. Or maybe it's through a service project you help with to bless someone you may never meet.

Whatever the case, Jesus wants to grow His love in your heart and watch it bloom as you become more and more like Him.

Heavenly Father, I can't believe You care about me as
much as You do. It's amazing that I matter to You and that
You want to be with me forever. Thank You, Jesus, for Your
love and everything You do for me. Help me to remember how
much You care so that I can be confident and a blessing to others.

HE UNDERSTANDS

*O Lord, You have looked through me and have
known me. You know when I sit down and when I
get up. You understand my thoughts from far away.*
Psalm 139:1–2

Do you ever dream about what you want to be when you grow up? Sometimes that can be a very hard decision to make. After high school, you might attend college with more classes and even more studying. Whether you become an astronaut or schoolteacher, firefighter or lawyer, author or artist, your first and biggest responsibility is to share the love and hope of Jesus.

Sharing Jesus with others is how you will be successful in your adventure to change the world. God understands your thoughts. He knows what makes you nervous, scared, or fearful. He made you and will always love you—even on days when you feel disconnected from Him.

Look for all the ways God is communicating with you, and be encouraged. Stars sprinkled across the heavens. Beautiful sunsets. Snowfalls. Spring flowers. Butterflies. Beaches. Consider how God made all these things special and unique. Then think about how much more special you are to Him. You matter to the King!

*Lord, I'm so humbled that You think I'm important. You made
me and understand everything I go through. Sometimes I
don't know why certain things happen, but I trust that You
have all the answers. Please keep leading the way.*

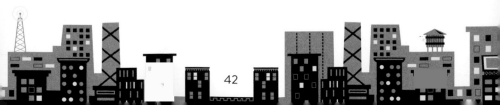

WITH YOU

"When you pass through the waters, I will be with you. When you pass through the rivers, they will not flow over you. When you walk through the fire, you will not be burned. The fire will not destroy you."

ISAIAH 43:2

God promises to be with you. Through every stressful day, you are covered by the Creator. Through waters of worry, rivers of regret, and fires of fear, God has your back. He will keep teaching you how to be confident in His never-ending love for you.

There may be things you don't feel comfortable doing. Maybe you aren't a social person. That's okay, because God will still use you even in situations where you don't feel confident. Rely on His truth that you are special, and He will always help you in every situation.

Think about how you can start to connect what God is teaching you in your quiet time to your new adventure of changing the world for His glory. Sometimes it may seem like your ideas won't work, but take them to Jesus. He will show you the path you should take. You will do great things for His glory!

Lord, thank You for promising me that You will always be faithful. Knowing Your presence is always with me brings me so much comfort. There's nowhere I can go that You won't be. I love You.

VIP

*The Spirit of the Lord God is on me, because the Lord
has chosen me to bring good news to poor people.*

ISAIAH 61:1

God made you to be important. Like today's scripture says, His Spirit is with you and He has planned for you to do really big things for His kingdom. Doing good things for others is something that God takes seriously. He wants to use you to help your friends understand that they matter to God.

You are important because you have the ability to use the Spirit's power to help people connect with Jesus. When you honor God, you open up a lot of doors for sharing His good news. Every chance you have to tell someone about Jesus is an opportunity to change someone's life forever!

Spend time thanking God for all the things He has given you. He loves you so much. He saved you. He chose you. He wants to use you to tell others about Jesus. Ask Him to show you His best plans for your life.

*Lord, most days I don't feel like I'm someone special. It feels like
I'm just going through the motions. Please help me think of others.
Make me bold enough to tell them You're the reason I care.*

GOD IS LISTENING

The Lord has heard my cry for help.
The Lord receives my prayer.
PSALM 6:9

Jesus hears you. Every time you talk to Him, He is listening. He loves you so much that even when you're *not* praying, He is ready and waiting to listen. He showers you with a love that fills your heart so that you never have to wonder if you matter to Him.

As you think about telling people in your world about Jesus, remember that you are filled with the Holy Spirit. This means that God has given you the power to be brave and confident. It's okay if you don't feel like you have all the right words. God does. It's okay if you don't feel like you are wise enough to share the gospel. God is. In these situations, pray and ask the Lord for the right words and wisdom to tell others about Jesus and the love He has for them.

God holds on to each word you lift up to Him. He doesn't let go of any of them—not one! He receives them. Then He provides for you and blesses you.

Jesus, please help me understand how awesome You are.
Thank You for hearing me. I'm so amazed by You and Your love.

FOREVER LOVE

Who can keep us away from the love of Christ? Can trouble or
problems? Can suffering wrong from others or having no food?
Can it be because of no clothes or because of danger or war?
ROMANS 8:35

God doesn't forget anything you tell Him. Some days may not go the way
you planned. You might feel disappointed or depressed. But Jesus wants
you to know that, because you mean so much to Him, He is always with you.

As you become a world changer, you will have difficulties. You might
try to tell a friend about Jesus, but they act like they're not interested. You
might try to read your Bible but find that you have a hard time connecting
with the Lord. You may feel overwhelmed and want to give up altogether.
These setbacks or bad feelings are not powerful enough to keep Jesus
away from you!

The Bible promises that not even suffering or war can come between
you and Jesus. Let that truth settle your soul. Let the Lord's promises calm
your anxiety. Receive peace and the Lord's forever love!

Jesus, I pray that You would help me trust You more. Help me
understand just how awesome and lasting Your love is. Thank You!

TRUSTING JESUS

I have been put up on the cross to die with Christ. I no longer live. Christ lives in me. The life I now live in this body, I live by putting my trust in the Son of God. He was the One Who loved me and gave Himself for me.
GALATIANS 2:20

When you share the message of God's love with the world, don't forget to keep your trust in Jesus. This is the key to becoming everything God made you to be. If your trust isn't in Jesus, then your trust will be in your own feelings, and you can't always count on your feelings. But you *can* count on Jesus!

Take Joseph, for example. His brothers sold him into slavery. In Egypt, he was put in prison for more than twelve years. Despite all the untrue accusations against him, Joseph kept his trust in God. Eventually, Joseph was released from prison and promoted to second-in-command under the pharaoh! He even saved his brothers and father by giving them food when they were in danger of starvation.

Is there a part of your day when you feel like you need to trust God more? Trust God to keep His promises to you. If you find yourself feeling anxious, ask the Lord for help. With His guidance, you will be able to trust that He always wants what's best for you!

Lord, I want to bring You glory through my actions. Help me trust You more and more each day. Help me know that You are in control of my life and that Your love will always be with me.

LEADING IN LOVE

May the Lord lead your hearts into the love of God.
May He help you as you wait for Christ.
2 THESSALONIANS 3:5

The Lord knows how much effort you're putting into your schoolwork. He's proud of you and wants you to keep going. Whether you know it or not, He is using you to be an example of His goodness. There are people around you who are struggling with many hard things. Your kind spirit will be a blessing to them, and that's part of your world-changing adventure.

When you make time to read God's Word every day, it will help you be led into His love. Then you can wait for Jesus to move. Moses was someone who talked with God and could hear His voice! Can you imagine? But even Moses had to wait. Forty years passed while Moses was a shepherd in a faraway land called Midian, and then Moses went back to Egypt to confront the pharaoh and eventually free the Israelites.

While you're going through your daily routine, pay attention to where the Lord is leading you. No matter what, God is proud of you and leading you in His unfailing love!

Lord, some days I don't feel connected to You. I know You're there, but sometimes I wish I could hear Your voice like Moses did. Please keep holding my hand and leading me.

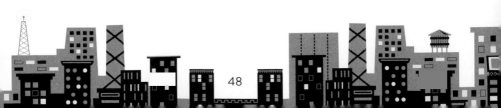

DON'T GIVE UP

*Let us keep looking to Jesus. Our faith comes from Him
and He is the One Who makes it perfect. He did not give
up when He had to suffer shame and die on a cross.*

Hebrews 12:2

Keep your eyes on Jesus. He's the one who gives you a strong faith. He teaches you how to trust Him and gives you strength to carry on, even on the hardest days. Remember how much you're loved—you can know it for sure, because Jesus didn't walk away when He was faced with the cross.

He endured the pain and humiliation and hardship because He cares so much about you. And even though you weren't born yet, He could look into the future and know how wonderful a relationship with you would be. To Jesus, you are worth everything He had to go through!

When it comes to sharing the good news of Jesus and His power to forgive sins, think about how you can tell others what He's done for you. It's easier than you think. Be brave. Be like Jesus. Maybe start with a friend. Tell your friend just how special Jesus is to you. When you do, you're not only honoring Jesus but also being a great friend.

*Lord, please give me the strength to be brave and to share the good
news of the cross with a friend. Your victory over sin and death is
the best thing I could ever share with my friend, and I don't want to
waste any time waiting. Help me make today count for Your glory!*

THE GIFT

*God has given each of you a gift. Use it to help
each other. This will show God's loving-favor.*
1 PETER 4:10

What do you like to do? Do you like to read books or solve puzzles? Do you like to talk to friends or play video games? How about playing sports? Whatever it is, God made you special. He gave you certain talents and skills and desires that no one else has.

When you start to be intentional and connect the things you like to do with ways that you can change the world, sharing the good news of Jesus becomes easier and more exciting. Your gifts and talents are great opportunities to be a blessing to other people.

The apostle Paul loved to talk. He had an outgoing personality, and no matter who he was with, Paul would always talk about Jesus. In fact, most of the New Testament was written by Paul. Even at the end of his life when he was a prisoner in Rome, Paul told people about Jesus. You also will do big things for God if you keep obeying His commands your whole life. Don't worry. Just take one step at a time matching your gifts to sharing the gospel, and you'll be on your way!

*Jesus, I haven't spent much time thinking about all the ways You have
made me special. Help me to do that. Please give me the wisdom to use
my gifts for Your glory. Show me how I can be a blessing to others.*

GO!

*He said to them, "You are to go to all the world
and preach the Good News to every person."*
MARK 16:15

You never know the impact you might have on a friend or a family member. Sometimes it may feel like you're just going through the motions and not making much of an impact, if any. But that's just not true. God promises to be with you always, and He also says that He has big plans for your life.

Over time, people will know that you are different because you live to honor Jesus—and it shows in the way you live your life. Finding ways to help other people and making it a habit to always use kind words will let others know that you are somebody who can be trusted. Once people get to know you, they will begin to listen to—and be interested in—what you have to say.

This makes for a great opportunity to talk about Jesus. It doesn't have to be awkward. You can be intentional about telling people about the blessings God has given you. Let them know how He takes good care of you, always providing for you, listening to you, and keeping His promises to you.

*Jesus, with Your help, I can make a positive impact
on others. Please open doors and give me the
courage to speak about Your holy name.*

THE WAY

Jesus said, "I am the Way and the Truth and the Life.
No one can go to the Father except by Me."
JOHN 14:6

The world is filled with many different religions. So many people don't believe in God or Jesus. They spend their days trying to find answers, but no matter what they do, they keep missing out on the truth. That's where *you* come in!

Your world-changing adventure focuses on Jesus. As the Bible says, He is the way—meaning He is the only way to God. He is also the truth—which means He is the answer to every single one of our problems. And finally, Jesus is life—He is the only way to have an abundant life now and an amazing life of connection with God eternally.

You have a very special calling. You have the opportunity, not only to change the world, but to change someone's life for all eternity. That's an awesome responsibility! Don't worry, because God is giving you everything you need to be successful. He has your back!

Lord, it's overwhelming to think that I have the ability
to help people connect with You and have a personal
relationship with You forever. Please bring me
opportunities to speak the truth. Thank You!

THE ENDS OF THE EARTH

"But you will receive power when the Holy Spirit comes into your life. You will tell about Me in the city of Jerusalem and over all the countries of Judea and Samaria and to the ends of the earth."

Acts 1:8

The Lord has given you the Holy Spirit, and the Spirit is powerful. He will guide you and teach you and lead you to live for God's glory. Even though you will run into challenges every day, you can feel confident that, with the Holy Spirit, everything will be okay.

The Holy Spirit is your number one resource to help you take the message of Jesus and His love to your neighborhood, your school, and all the other places you might go. Wherever you are right now, the Lord is opening doors of opportunity for you to be brave and tell people about Him.

Thinking about how much Jesus loves you will motivate you to tell others how awesome He is. The Bible says that God loves the world, and that's why He sent Jesus to save us. When Jesus was on the cross, He thought about you as much as He thought of every other person on earth.

Jesus, thank You for saving me and calling me to share Your message of love. And thank You for the Holy Spirit You've given me to help me boldly share Your name. I pray that I will be faithful to the job You've given me to do. In Your holy name I pray. Amen.

SEND ME

Then I heard the voice of the Lord, saying, "Whom should I send?
Who will go for Us?" Then I said, "Here am I. Send me!"
ISAIAH 6:8

Having a willing heart is the key to maximizing your world-changing adventure. Sometimes when your parents ask you to do something, you may not want to do it. But you know, deep down in your heart, that being respectful and doing what you're asked is always the best way to go. Not only does it honor your parents, but it also brings glory to God.

The prophet Isaiah is a great example of someone who loved the Lord and had a willing heart. He told God that no matter what, he wanted to go and speak the truth to as many people as would listen. The book of Isaiah is filled with amazing promises and proof of just how much God cares for you and all of His people.

Don't wait around for someone else to tell you what to do when it comes to sharing your faith. Stay connected to God through prayer and follow His lead. Tell God the same thing that Isaiah told Him: "Here am I. Send me!" When you're ready, you'll be amazed at how many opportunities God brings your way!

Thank You, Lord, for using me. I know I'm not the smartest or strongest,
but none of this is about me anyway. All of my life, my job is to help
make You famous, and I am blessed to be a part of that adventure!

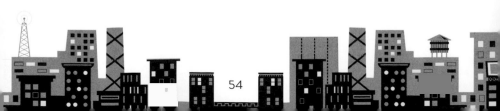

BLESS THE NATIONS

"Go and make followers of all the nations. Baptize them in the name of the Father and of the Son and of the Holy Spirit."
MATTHEW 28:19

Jesus told His disciples to tell the world about Him. He told them to go out and make followers from the people who lived near and far. One day, believers all over the world will praise His holy name together—in celebration of His love and salvation! It's amazing to think that what began with only thirteen people—Jesus and His disciples—is now a worldwide family of brothers and sisters in Christ.

A lot of grown-ups go on mission trips with their churches to places where people may not have heard of the name of Jesus. Some of those trips include service projects and prayer meetings, but whatever the case, the number one feature of all of them is relationship building.

Whether you go on a mission trip to the other end of the map or just tell a friend about Jesus, God is equally proud of your efforts to make His name famous. Just remember to keep going and always be on the lookout for opportunities to change the world. Tell people a message that will change their hearts forever!

Lord God, I need help with so many things, but right now I ask that You would help me be active in sharing my faith. Help me to be brave and always focused on the goal, no matter where I am.

HARVESTTIME

Jesus said to them, "There is much grain ready to gather. But the workmen are few. Pray then to the Lord Who is the Owner of the grain-fields that He will send workmen to gather His grain."

LUKE 10:2

The Lord is so good. It can't be said enough: He loves you and thinks you're wonderful! After all, He made you in His image. Let that truth encourage you. Let it fill your heart and soul and spirit as you consider all the ways you can change the world for Jesus.

So many people are waiting to hear the good news of Jesus. That's why you are so important to this world-changing adventure! You have a story the world needs to hear—the story of how Jesus saved you and changed your life forever.

So many people who believe in Jesus get too wrapped up in their daily lives to even consider telling other people about Him. You will never reach a point where you've shared the good news with too many people. There will always be new people who need to hear the salvation story. Keep sharing throughout your whole life. Stay connected to the Lord. Go about the business of the harvest.

*Jesus, I ask that You would help me find
new people to tell about Your salvation.*

MESSAGE OF HOPE

*I am not ashamed of the Good News. It is the power
of God. It is the way He saves men from the punishment of their sins if they put their trust in Him.*
ROMANS 1:16

Words are powerful things. When you compliment someone, your words
make them feel good. On the other hand, when somebody says something
mean, those words hurt people's feelings. The Bible says that when we tell
people the good news of Jesus, God's power flows through our words.

Remember that every time you share your testimony and treat others
the way Jesus would treat them, you are glorifying God. Jesus is the only
one who can save us from our sins. Reminding people that their hard work
and good deeds aren't enough helps them understand they need to put all
their trust in Jesus.

Spreading the Lord's message of hope everywhere you go sows seeds
of love and righteousness. Allow the Lord to work through you so that your
world-changing adventure will bless many lives and open doors for others
to feel the unending love that Jesus has for them.

*Jesus, thank You for saving me. Thank You for letting me be a
part of Your world-changing adventure. I pray that You would
lead me to people who desperately need to feel Your love.*

COME, FOLLOW ME

Jesus said to them, "Follow Me. I will make you fish for men!"
MATTHEW 4:19

When Jesus started His earthly ministry, He worked with people who weren't famous or even popular. Some of them were fishermen. And when Jesus called them, He said He had a much more important job for them to do. He told them they would fish for people—meaning they would tell others about Jesus and the gift of eternal life.

Believe it or not, Jesus is calling you to the same adventure. He wants you to fish for people too! Jesus wants you to put Him first and follow Him. When you walk behind Him and let Him lead the way, your gospel sharing will be super effective. Following Jesus will help you stay on track with His plans for your life.

People are—and always have been—the biggest priority to Jesus. He endured the suffering of the cross so people could have hope and faith and know they can always rely on Him. You will probably never know all the things a person is going through, but you can be certain that telling them about Jesus will help them through life's hard times.

Jesus, thank You for saving me when I couldn't save myself. I ask that You keep making me brave so I will continue to follow You no matter where You lead me.

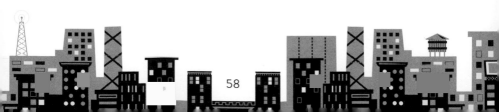

GOD'S PERFECT WORD

All the Holy Writings are God-given and are made alive by Him. Man is helped when he is taught God's Word. It shows what is wrong. It changes the way of a man's life. It shows him how to be right with God.
2 Timothy 3:16

The Bible is an amazing book. It's not just words on a page with some nice stories—it is God-breathed and alive! It's the living Word of God! It has the power to transform lives forever. It has the power to motivate and heal hearts.

As you set out to change the world and make Jesus famous, remember that the Bible is your anchor. It will keep you secure and connected to God's truth. As you read the true stories of men and women who loved the Lord—like Esther, Joseph, Noah, Abraham, and Mary, God will remind you that you too are on your way to doing big things for His kingdom.

Today, make a plan to read your Bible every day. This regular quiet time with Jesus is so important! Don't only sit and read (and think about) His words to you, but also be quiet and listen for His voice. He'll teach you new and wonderful things!

Dear Jesus, I'm sorry that I don't read my Bible as much as I should. Please open my eyes and heart to experience Your words in a brand-new way.

STANDING AT THE DOOR

"See! I stand at the door and knock. If anyone hears My voice and opens the door, I will come in to him and we will eat together."
REVELATION 3:20

Jesus is always there for you. In the book of Revelation, Jesus reminds us that He stands at the doors of our hearts and knocks. Part of this means He's trying to get the attention of people who don't know Him; but this is also a great reminder that Jesus wants to have a deep, loving relationship with you every day of your life. He wants to spend time with you!

The Lord is never far away from you. Throughout your day, slow down enough to listen for His voice. You'll be able to hear Him call—not out loud like you would hear a friend on the phone, but more like you can hear the wind on a breezy day. Your heart will be able to hear the Lord say, "I love you."

Think about something you might be doing that you could do better. Maybe you aren't as respectful as you should be when your parents ask you to do your chores. Your disrespect is like a closed door. And when you open the door and let Jesus come in, you're welcoming Him and asking Him to help you be respectful in that situation. Letting Jesus come into the parts of your life where you may be a little selfish allows Him to take over and help you become more like Him.

Dear Jesus, thank You for knocking on the door of my heart. I pray for strength to open every closed door, because I want You to come in and change my heart.

BEST NEWS OF ALL

So Philip started with this part of the Holy Writings
and preached the Good News of Jesus to him.
ACTS 8:35

Maybe a friend invites you to an epic birthday party. Or maybe your parents come home and announce that you're going on a long-awaited vacation. Or maybe you get news that a gift you've always wanted is on the way. Although all of those things are fantastic, the very best news of all is that Jesus died for your sins and loves you so much that He wants to be with you forever.

There was a man named Philip who loved the Lord. He had the opportunity to share the best news of all with a stranger. (The story is found in your Bible in Acts 8.) Afterward, the stranger put his faith in Jesus and was even baptized. The coolest part is that the man was full of joy—the kind of joy that can come only from a Jesus-filled heart.

As you stay committed to reading your Bible and learning more and more about how awesome Jesus is, get ready for your own "Philip experience." It doesn't matter how young or old you are—God will use you to share the best news of all.

Jesus, thank You for the story of Philip and how he helped change
a stranger's life forever. Philip was brave enough to tell a stranger
about You, Lord. Please help me do the same. Help me be more
and more like You so Your love will overflow in my life.

THINGS THAT LAST

"He who puts his trust in the Son has life that lasts forever."
JOHN 3:36

Everything in life eventually wears out. The tires on your parents' car will need to be replaced. If you wear glasses, you'll eventually need a new prescription. The shoes on your feet will eventually wear out, and you'll find yourself in need of new ones. Things wearing out is just a fact of life.

But. . .Jesus came and offered everyone a new hope—eternal life with Him in heaven. That promise lasts forever; it will never wear out. People spend so much time trying to find ways to be happy in the world. Trips, video games, food, books—they all bring a certain level of happiness. But the problem is these things don't last. The trips come to an end, the video game gets old and boring, you eventually get hungry for food again, and every book has an ending.

Jesus is calling you to invest your time in the one thing that lasts. Think about ways you can show Jesus to the people around you. Show grace even when it's hard. Extend forgiveness even when it feels impossible. The more you act like Jesus, the more willing people will be to listen to what you have to say.

Lord, I am so grateful You have given me the gift of eternal life. Help me work to grow Your kingdom. Help me remind people of the most important thing in life—You!

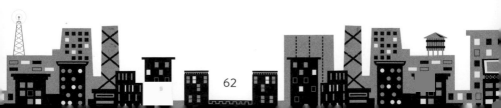

FIRST OF ALL

"The Good News must first be preached to all the nations."
MARK 13:10

So many people in the world haven't heard about Jesus. Others have heard His name but have never really been told who He is. You can help with this! As you head out on your world-changing adventure, you can help others see Jesus in your behavior.

Jesus said that before He returns, a message of salvation—the salvation that only He offers—will be preached throughout the entire world. This doesn't mean you have to get on an airplane and travel all over the world telling as many people as you can about the Lord. But you can do your part right where you are—right in your own little corner of the world.

You never know if the friend you tell about Jesus today will go home and then share your story with his grandparent who lives in a different state. Then that grandparent shares the story of Jesus with a neighbor. The neighbor has a sister who lives in a different country. The sister then shares the story of Jesus where she lives. This kind of thing can really happen! So you see. . .your boldness can literally turn into a world-changing event!

Jesus, I don't always feel like I can make a difference
in the world. But I know You are capable of anything,
so I pray You would give me the strength and wisdom and
courage I need to take that first step of faith.

TELL THE WORLD

Tell of His shining-greatness among the nations.
Tell of His wonderful works among all the people.
PSALM 96:3

Before you begin to share the gospel with someone, think about how awesome Jesus is and all the wonderful things He has done for you. This way, you will have some excitement blended in with your story. If you're excited, the person who's listening won't be able to help but consider Jesus.

The Lord wants us to care about all people regardless of their background or beliefs. When we care about *all* people, we are not only being obedient to His Word but also creating deep, trustworthy relationships. If your friend who doesn't know Jesus hears you talking about the gospel—and you've proved how much you care about them—they are more likely to lean in and really listen to what you have to say.

If it's helpful, grab a journal or a notebook and start listing all your blessings that have come from the Lord. From the food in your refrigerator to the clothes on your back to your books and toys and other great things, Jesus has provided it all. And that's a great thing to remember as you go and share the good news. Jesus gave it all on the cross, and He provides it all now.

Jesus, thank You for all the ways You bless me and my family.
Life would be miserable without You. Help me have a grateful
heart. Help me develop good, trusting relationships with the
people around me. Help me be a good listener, and then give
me courage to tell people about Your goodness and love.

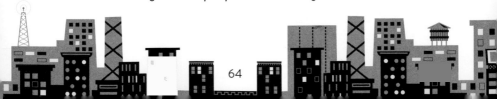

LIVING AND POWERFUL

God's Word is living and powerful. It is sharper than a
sword that cuts both ways. It cuts straight into where
the soul and spirit meet and it divides them.

HEBREWS 4:12

You already know God's Word is powerful. And not only is it powerful, but it's "living"—meaning that it leads you and teaches you and shows you the right way to live your life. The writer of Hebrews describes the Bible as the sharpest of swords, able to cut into our spiritual beings so the truth of God is planted deep within our souls.

Not only is the Bible filled with directions and guidance, but it is also God's letter of love to His children. The examples of God's love in the Bible are too numerous to count, but as you read them, you're reminded of how important you are to Him. You're also reminded of how special and unique and wonderful He made you. Before you took your first breath, God knew you and He loved you!

As you grow in your faith and walk with Jesus, ask Him to help you see your Bible as a great treasure. Read it daily. Let God's words fill your mind and heart with reminders of His love.

Father God, help me see my Bible in a brand-new way.
Help me understand just how amazing it is. As I reread Your
words, I pray that they will teach me new lessons and remind
me of what an amazing promise keeper You are.

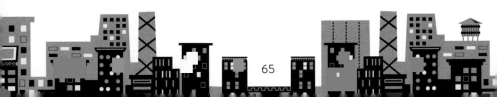

ON A MISSION

We are Christ's missionaries. God is speaking to you through us. We are speaking for Christ and we ask you from our hearts to turn from your sins and come to God.

2 CORINTHIANS 5:20

If you think of the word *missionary*, you might think of people who go to the farthest parts of the world and live in tents in the jungle. Although some missionaries may go to remote parts of the world to share the gospel with strangers, the Lord wants you to know that you too can be a missionary right where you live.

Right where you are, you can speak for Jesus. God speaks through you to help other people know more about His one and only Son. Your sharing of the good news of what Jesus has done for people can even come through your actions and not just through your words. It's important to remember to always treat people with respect and kindness.

Each day of your world-changing journey gives you an opportunity to be a missionary for Jesus. Remember that your life brings Jesus glory—so whether you're at school or at home or at the store or at practice, you are being a missionary when you act like Jesus. Make the most of the opportunities you're given to share Jesus in as many places as possible.

Lord, I've never really thought about becoming a missionary when I grow up. And even though I may never get on a plane and go overseas when I'm older, I'm never too young to start being a missionary right here where I live. Help me make Your name famous.

FOR EVERYONE

*He paid for our sins with His own blood. He did not pay
for ours only, but for the sins of the whole world.*

1 JOHN 2:2

When you have your next quiet time with Jesus, try to grasp exactly what He did for you. Because of our sins, a sacrifice had to be made for us to be able to stand before our holy and perfect God. God thought about you and everyone else and decided to send His Son to earth as a living sacrifice so we could have our sins forgiven.

Jesus died even for people who reject Him. So it's important to share Jesus with everyone you know—your family, friends, and neighbors. That's your job; the Lord's job is doing the saving. Sometimes it's easy to tell our friends about Jesus, but when we think of telling people we don't know, it can seem a bit scary.

To share Jesus, you don't have to love talking in front of people and you certainly don't have to know all the answers. All you need to do is be faithful. When an opportunity presents itself, be brave and share a blessing or two. Sometime during your conversations with others, the Lord will give you a chance to speak truth. You've got this!

*Lord, thank You for the sacrifice You made on the cross.
Keep me humble as I try to tell as many people as I can about
what You've done for them too. Help me have compassion
for everyone, not just the people who are easy to talk to.*

GREAT RICHES

*I was to tell them of the great riches in
Christ which do not come to an end.*

EPHESIANS 3:8

The Lord has so many blessings in store for you. He loves you and cares for you deeply. The Bible reminds us that Jesus is always with us, and the blessings He offers last forever.

When you think about heaven, remember that Jesus told His friends that He was going to prepare a place for them and then He would come back for His people. No one knows exactly when He will return, but the fact that He *will* return should encourage us to live lives that bring Him glory.

You can bring Him glory by helping a friend ask Jesus into their heart, or by being helpful and encouraging to someone who needs it. These things show others the love of Jesus. In return, Jesus holds you close and blesses you. He reminds you that you're His precious child.

Your relationship with the Lord will never end! Each new day that He gives you is a chance for you to read more of His Word and make choices that line up with His plans for your life. Being with Jesus every day doesn't mean you will never have problems, but it does mean that you will always be taken care of. Jesus promises never to leave your side, and He will always guide you. Rely on Him and His never-ending goodness.

I need more of You, Jesus. I admit I get distracted sometimes and forget that You're right here with me. Show me how to act and how to make good decisions that bring You glory. Help me make my life one big worship service that praises Your holy name.

PREACH!

So then, faith comes to us by hearing the Good News.
And the Good News comes by someone preaching it.
ROMANS 10:17

Jesus could have snapped His fingers from heaven and treated people like robots, making them believe in Him just like that. But because He loves us so much, He wants to have a close relationship with us—a relationship that we choose.

Jesus made it a priority to build relationships with people. When you read your Bible, you can feel the love of Jesus rising off the page and planting itself in your heart. We're told in Romans 10:17 that when we preach the good news, we give others an opportunity to hear it—and then they have the opportunity to ask Jesus to be the Lord of their life.

Don't ever think that you are bothering people when you tell them about Jesus. If you don't tell them about Him, who will? Start changing the world right where you are, starting with the relationships you already have. Don't forget that you have the Holy Spirit to give you power and strength to go and share the good news!

Jesus, I don't feel like there are many people I can tell
about Your saving grace. Please help me be aware of
people around me who need to hear about the amazing
hope and peace that are found in a relationship with You.

THE POWERFUL CROSS

*Preaching about the cross sounds foolish to those who
are dying in sin. But it is the power of God to those of
us who are being saved from the punishment of sin.*
1 CORINTHIANS 1:18

When you share Jesus, always remember that the central message of the good news is the work He did on the cross. He was unjustly condemned to death and nailed to a criminal's cross to become our perfect sacrifice.

There will be people who hear your message and dismiss it, but that's okay. The apostle Paul said the good news might sound silly to those who don't understand what Jesus did for them. Don't let that stop you from doing God's work. There is great power in the cross. Let it remind you of the love that the Lord has for you and all His people.

Sometimes people think if they're good enough or work hard enough they can earn favor with God, but sadly that isn't the case. There are many good people in the world who are dying in their sins because they don't have a relationship with Jesus. Rely on the powerful cross of Jesus. Let it motivate you to go out and change your world. The people who receive your message of hope and put their trust in Jesus will never be the same again. What wonderful news!

*Lord, thank You for taking my place on the cross. I wish You
wouldn't have had to endure so much suffering, but I am
grateful You chose to so that I can spend forever with You.*

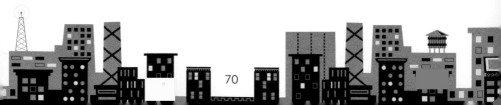

SHINING LIGHTS

The eyes of those who do not believe are made blind by Satan who is the god of this world. He does not want the light of the Good News to shine in their hearts. This Good News shines as the shining-greatness of Christ.
2 CORINTHIANS 4:4

As a believer in Jesus, you are to be a light in the world. Our world is filled with darkness that keeps people's minds off God. Being a light for Jesus, giving hope to people who need it, is one of the best ways to change the world.

If you've ever seen a lighthouse, you know they were built to help ships safely reach the shore. Ship captains had books that were filled with the locations of all the lighthouses and the unique markings on them. When they saw the lighthouses as they navigated their ships, they were able to determine their location. It's kind of the same thing for believers. As a light for Jesus, you should stand out in the crowd so the people who are looking for answers will gravitate toward you. Then they can hear your good news about Jesus.

While we work on shining our lights, the enemy tries to keep people in the dark. He doesn't want them to seek out a relationship with Jesus. When you shine your light of faith brightly, you are helping people see the real love of Jesus!

Lord, I want to be a bright light in this world. I want to share Your message of hope so others will look to You and experience Your amazing love.

NO PRIDE

*I cannot be proud because I preach the Good News.
I have been told to do it. It would be bad for
me if I do not preach the Good News.*
1 CORINTHIANS 9:16

Pride can be a good thing—like when you hear someone say they take pride in their work. That means they care about doing a good job. But pride is not good when people start to think they are better than everyone else because of their accomplishments. When it comes to telling people about Jesus, we should never be prideful.

Being humble is the opposite of thinking you're better than others. Being humble is acting like Jesus—by putting other people first and having compassion for what others are going through. When you're humble, people are more likely to trust you when you talk to them about important things, like the good news of Jesus.

Jesus wants us to tell people how much He loves them, and being humble helps open doors for genuine conversations with friends and family. Think about your day and consider ways you can have a humble attitude. And then try it out. You'll be surprised at how contagious your humility becomes to the people around you.

*Lord, help me remember that You are the reason for every
blessing in my life. Help me avoid being prideful. Keep me
humble and give me a heart willing to serve others.*

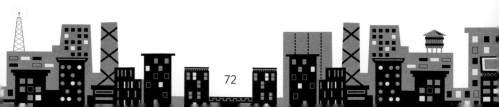

ALWAYS

Preach the Word of God. Preach it when it is easy and people want to listen and when it is hard and people do not want to listen. Preach it all the time.

2 Timothy 4:2

Sometimes it's hard to do the right thing. The Bible teaches us that sharing the love of Jesus is something we should be doing all the time. Sharing the love of Jesus can be as simple as being a good friend to those around you.

When you share the gospel, your actions are just as powerful as your words. The Bible includes a true story about a lady named Mary. She had a sister named Martha. Both sisters loved Jesus. And one day Jesus came to visit them. Martha kept herself busy doing things, while Mary decided to sit at the feet of Jesus and listen to what He had to say. Martha got mad at her sister for not helping her around the house, but Jesus said Mary understood what was most important.

Being a good preacher of the good news means you need to spend time sitting at the feet of Jesus—by reading your Bible every day and paying attention to everything God has to teach you. Don't let busyness or laziness distract you from doing the work you've been called to do. Always look for ways to be a light and share the love of Jesus.

Jesus, I pray for many opportunities to share Your love with other people. Whether it's hard or easy, I pray that I would be faithful to share the good news.

OPEN THEIR EYES

"You are to open their eyes. You are to turn them from darkness to light. You are to turn them from the power of Satan to the power of God."
ACTS 26:18

The Bible tells about a man named Paul who went on a world-changing adventure. At first, Paul made a lot of bad decisions. Then he had an encounter with Jesus and his whole life was turned upside down—in a very good way! Jesus told Paul that he had a new job to do. Jesus wanted Paul to be a witness to the world so people would come to know Jesus and turn from darkness. Jesus sent Paul out into the world so that people could come to believe in Jesus, receive forgiveness of their sins, and live with Him forever.

The interesting thing about Paul's story is that some people truly thought he was out of his mind. But Paul remained faithful to his Savior and didn't let anything keep him from bringing glory to God. The enemy doesn't want people to know they are loved by Jesus. He will do whatever it takes to make people feel alone and unwanted—but the truth is, Jesus' love is more powerful than the enemy's darkness and lies. Be brave. Keep on sharing the love of Jesus in your world.

Father God, thank You for the story of Paul. Help me to be brave like he was and tell people about Your love. Don't let anything get in the way of me sharing You with the world.

PRECIOUS CHILD

*See what great love the Father has for us that He
would call us His children. And that is what we are.*

1 JOHN 3:1

If you go outside at night and look up at the stars, you can't help but think of God and His infinite creativity. Beyond the stars, think about planets, galaxies, the universe! It's all so mind-blowing. And the cool part is that the same one who created all those things also created you.

God calls you His child! Can you believe it? You are loved so much by the Creator that He sees you as His precious child. And He wants you to see Him as your loving Father. You can talk to Him whenever you need help. He is the best Father you could ever hope for!

When you look at your life from this perspective, every day becomes a gift—a celebration of the one who made you and loves you more than anything or anyone! Let the excitement of this truth fill your heart, mind, and soul. Let it motivate you to go out and change the world with the message of the heavenly Father's saving power.

*Dear Father, I can't believe You love me so much and that You
know me so deeply. Thank You, Lord. Please remind me how
special our relationship is on days when I forget. I love You!*

WALKING IN TRUTH

For Your loving-kindness is always in front
of my eyes. And I have walked in Your truth.
PSALM 26:3

Today is a brand-new day that the Lord has given you to do great things for His glory. It may seem like you're in a routine of doing schoolwork and chores—and while those things are important, you are also called to be a light for Jesus. Be intentional about ways you can bless others. This is where God is leading you.

The Bible tells about a man named Matthew whom Jesus called to be one of His disciples. Matthew had been a tax collector for the Romans, a job that wasn't very respected. When Matthew met Jesus, he stopped being a tax collector and followed the Lord because he saw something different in the Savior's eyes. Instead of collecting taxes, he traveled and shared the good news. He helped to show others the Lord's amazing love.

Like Matthew, today you are walking in truth. Make good choices. Bring honor to your Lord. When you share His love, you're helping others to walk in truth as well.

Jesus, thank You for calling me out of my selfish life and into
Your loving arms. I pray that my actions would show other
people what a relationship with You can do for their hearts.

FINISH THE RACE

"But I am not worried about this. I do not think of my life as worth much, but I do want to finish the work the Lord Jesus gave me to do. My work is to preach the Good News of God's loving-favor."
ACTS 20:24

The Lord doesn't want you to worry about anything. He made you unique and for a purpose. Out of all the people in the world, there's only one you—and that makes you pretty special in the Lord's eyes. Be brave. Use your unique gifts to help share the good news.

You will change the world when you share the message of the Lord's loving-kindness. When you tell others about the love Jesus has for them, you are doing the work that the Lord has called you to do. Knowing that God has called you to do His work should give you confidence and a renewed spirit.

Over and over again in the Bible, God tells His people not to be afraid. That's because He is bigger than all your problems put together, and He always will be! He spoke the world into existence. He breathed His breath and formed you into being. The same power that did all that is also in you. You can move mountains in faith as you go and tell people about your awesome God.

Jesus, thank You for letting me be a part of Your plan to change the world. I can't do anything on my own. Help me not to worry. Help me to be strong and finish the jobs You are calling me to do. I pray that others will see You in my actions and words. Amen.

YOU ARE LOVED

"The Father loves you. He loves you because you
love Me and believe that I came from the Father."
JOHN 16:27

You are so loved and adored by the Creator of the universe that there are not enough words to describe just how deep and amazing and true His love for you is.

God wants you to be with Him forever, so He sent His only Son, Jesus, to come into the world and eventually give His life on the cross so you could have a way to be saved. His love is unbelievable, really, because the Bible tells us in Romans 5:8 that God the Father and Jesus the Son did all this when we were still lost in the mire of our sins. We didn't do anything to earn God's love. He just loves us—no strings attached! Don't ever forget how much you mean to Jesus.

Spend your days getting to know Jesus better. Keep believing that He wants only the best for you and that His plans are perfect. Even on the days when things don't seem to be going your way, remember that you mean the world to Jesus and that His love for you will not only fill your heart but light your way *forever*!

- -

Dear heavenly Father, I can't believe You love me so much.
I love You too, Lord, and I'm so grateful You care about me.
Thank You for everything You've done for me already—and
for all the things You will do for me in the future. Thank
You for holding on to me and never letting go!

STAY AND WAIT

Keep yourselves in the love of God. Wait for life that lasts forever through the loving-kindness of our Lord Jesus Christ.
JUDE 1:21

Sometimes waiting is super hard. Maybe there's something you've been wanting for a long time and it seems like you're never going to get it. Don't lose hope. The Lord wants you to know how much He loves you—so that while you're waiting, you'll know He's right there beside you, encouraging you and giving you patience.

It's hard to be patient. But know you're never alone. Jesus is working with you through all the ups and downs. He will never leave your side. As you make plans to share His message of hope with other people, stay in His love and wait for Him to guide you.

Staying and waiting doesn't mean you do nothing. It just means you take plenty of quiet time to hang out in the Lord's presence. You pray for opportunities to make Him famous. Don't forget how proud He is of you. Listen and you'll hear Him say, "Well done, child."

Jesus, it's hard to wait. There are some things I've been praying for that haven't happened yet. I'm trying to be patient. Help me stay close to You while I wait. Please take away my anxiety. Thank You for loving me. In Your holy name, I pray.

GOD'S GREAT GIFT

*Of what great worth is Your loving-kindness, O God! The children
of men come and are safe in the shadow of Your wings.*
PSALM 36:7

Putting your faith in the promises of God each day is a great way to live.
God wants you to understand what a treasure you are to Him and what a
treasure His love is to you. Your connection to Him is powerful. You share
a loving bond that is the basis for your entire world-changing journey.

God keeps you safe even when things feel like they're falling apart.
The Bible uses the phrase "in the shadow of His wings" to explain how
God's love covers us no matter what situation we're in. You might be
familiar with the man named Jonah in the Bible who ran away from God.
God kept calling him, and Jonah kept running away. It wasn't until he got
swallowed by a huge fish that he realized how much God loved him and
cared about him.

Let God's great gift of love for you fill your heart and soul so that you
always know how much you mean to Him. Rely on the Lord's strength to
stay connected with Him and His Word. Let your light shine in this dark
and broken world.

*Jesus, I need You so much. Nothing in this world
means more to me than You. Thank You for all the
different ways You shower me with Your love!*

HELP!

Help me, O Lord my God!
Save me by Your loving-kindness.
PSALM 109:26

The Lord is always there to help you. Whether it's to calm your heart when you feel anxious or to give you encouragement to accomplish a big task, the Lord is ready to help you. His love saves you from feeling alone and unwanted. You may have days when you don't feel like anyone understands what you're going through, but God does!

Make it a habit to talk to the Lord every day and share with Him all the things that are on your heart. Also make time to sit and listen. Think about all the ways Jesus has blessed you. Ask Him for help in dealing with other people and getting your schoolwork done, and thank Him for teaching you important lessons from the Bible.

God sent Moses to free His people from Egypt where they were being held captive. Moses didn't think he was able to do the job and asked God for help. (Read the full story in Exodus 3.) In the end, God was always there for Moses even when Moses didn't see it. It's the same for you today. Rely on God's help, and you will move mountains in faith!

Jesus, I need Your help. I need You to help me be a more caring person. Help me serve with a grateful heart. Thank You for always caring about me.

BIG PLANS

" 'For I know the plans I have for you,' says the Lord, 'plans for well-being and not for trouble, to give you a future and a hope.' "
JEREMIAH 29:11

It's awesome that God thinks about you all the time. He has plans that He designed especially for you and no one else. And when He created those plans, He made sure they were the very best plans for you.

God's plans are one of the ways He proves His love for you. Think about Noah in the book of Genesis. He built the ark and brought all the animals on board so that when the big flood came, they would be saved. Noah's seemingly crazy construction project made him the target of his neighbors' mockery and scorn. Nonetheless, he knew God had a plan for him and his family, and so he was obedient. At first, it probably seemed like a whole lot of hard work for nothing, but Noah kept his faith in the promise keeper.

You probably know the rest of the story. The entire earth was flooded, but Noah, his family, and the animals were safe inside the boat. As they were floating on the waters, Noah must have realized God's plan was awesome, although at times it was probably hard to understand. The ark provided hope and made a way for Noah and his family to have a good future in a brand-new place. And it's the same for you—God is working out great things for your life!

Jesus, please show me how to follow Your plans for my life.
In the middle of Your will is right where I want to be.

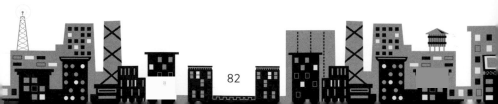

GIVE IT ALL

*No one can have greater love
than to give his life for his friends.*
JOHN 15:13

Jesus is the perfect example of giving away your life for your friends. He spent all His time loving and healing and teaching others. Jesus didn't just keep to Himself, but instead sought out people and took care of them. Jesus made sure He put others first.

When you work on reorganizing your priorities and look for ways to put other people first, you will begin to notice a change in your spirit. You will begin to feel a deeper connection with the Lord because You'll understand just how much He cares about everyone. He doesn't want you worrying about things. Instead, God wants you to trust that He has your back and is always making sure you have what you need.

When you seek to give your life away to help your friends and your parents, siblings, and other family members, you are making great use of the time the Lord has given you. As you start serving others, sharing the gospel story becomes more natural—and the people you're helping will be more willing to listen.

Lord, thank You for giving me all I need, and thank You for giving up Your life for me. Help me give my life away so I can help people turn from their selfishness and set their eyes on You!

RICH IN GOODNESS

*But You, O Lord, are a God full of love and pity. You are
slow to anger and rich in loving-kindness and truth.*
Psalm 86:15

God is always described as being rich in kindness and love. Spend some time thinking about all the ways God is good to you. You'll be amazed at how giving He is. The enemy, meanwhile, wants to keep our minds fearful and worried. When we're anxious, we tend to stop listening to God and try to fix problems ourselves.

When you read in the Bible that God has pity on His people, that means He is patient and understands us, especially when we're going through hard times. If you are going through a hard time, tell God all about it. He wants to know everything that bothers you and everything that makes you happy. God wants you to rely on Him for everything.

Let God's love for you be the encouragement you need every day. Let it fill your heart and overflow so that you can share His love with others. Whether it's in the kind words you say or your helpful acts of kindness, people will see a difference in you. They will open the doors for you to share the good news of Jesus!

*Jesus, I want to act like You more and more every day. Help me
rely on Your love and truth. Help me remember that You are
always in control and always want what's best for me.*

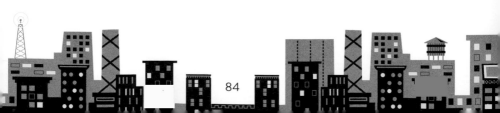

A THANKFUL HEART

Give thanks to the God of heaven,
for His loving-kindness lasts forever.
PSALM 136:26

God promises to always be with you and never leave you alone. When you fully understand His commitment to you, it should be easy to have a thankful heart for all He's done and all He will do for you.

You've probably met people who complain about everything. It's like nothing is ever good enough. That's the opposite of how Jesus wants us to be. Looking for things to be upset about keeps your heart from worshipping Jesus, because your focus is on the wrong things. God created us to connect with people in positive ways. Since your goal is to change the world for Him, the ability to view things from His perspective will be super helpful.

John the Baptist is a fantastic example of someone who was thankful. Day after day he told people about Jesus and baptized them. He lived out in the desert and wore strange clothes and ate bugs. But those things didn't matter to John because he was right in the middle of what God wanted him to do—and that alone was enough to fill his heart. He was rewarded when he looked up one day and saw Jesus standing there waiting to be baptized too!

Lord, thank You for all the ways You reach out and touch my heart. You've done so many things for me, and I pray that You would help me remember them so that I can live each day praising You instead of complaining.

DEAR JESUS

God had so much loving-kindness. He loved us with such a great love. Even when we were dead because of our sins, He made us alive by what Christ did for us. You have been saved from the punishment of sin by His loving-favor.
EPHESIANS 2:4–5

God is so awesome! He calls you His precious child and showers you with unfailing, unending, overwhelming love. There isn't enough room on a book's page to describe just how much He cares for and loves you.

He loves you so much that He gives you new life in Jesus. When you accept His free gift of salvation (through Jesus' sacrifice on the cross), you receive this new life. And this means you're a missionary now! A light shining in the dark world. You are on your way to do amazing things because of your relationship with Jesus.

The Lord will always show you favor. He will open doors. He will love you and bless you forever, because that's who He is. God will always chase after you even when you might feel like He's far away. He promises never to leave your side, and you can count on Him to help you anytime you call out to Him.

Jesus, I can never thank You enough for all You've done for me. Thank You for loving me so much and taking care of me. I love You.

PEACE BE WITH YOU

"The mountains may be taken away and the hills may shake, but My loving-kindness will not be taken from you. And My agreement of peace will not be shaken," says the Lord who has loving-pity on you.
ISAIAH 54:10

God is always on your side. He will never ever leave you alone. No matter how hard your day might be, He's always there, loving you and giving you peace.

When you have God's peace, you're able to rely on His truth in the hardest times. The Bible includes a story about the disciples that shows this kind of peace. The disciples were out on the lake in a boat when a storm hit. Jesus was sleeping in the stern of the boat, and His friends were scared. They woke Him up and asked how He could sleep in the middle of a storm like that. The cool thing about this story is that Jesus reminded them that He is the one who controls the wind and the waves. Jesus spoke and the storm stopped, the wind died down, and the sea grew calm. The disciples stood in awe.

This same powerful peace is for you too, brave boy! When things don't seem to be going the way you planned and you start to feel worried or afraid, remember that Jesus is with you and He's in control of everything!

Lord, thank You for Your ability to control the wind and the waves—and all the other things that happen in my life. Please help me to concentrate on Your love, especially when times get tough.

A FATHER'S LOVE

*"I have loved you just as My Father
has loved Me. Stay in My love."*
JOHN 15:9

It's exciting to know that Jesus loves you like God the Father loves Him. It's a love that cannot be explained or understood completely here on earth. It's a love that surrounds you, guides you, and fills your heart every second of every day of your life!

Make it a habit to think about this truth everywhere you go. It will change your life forever. The King of kings loves you and will always love you! You are a precious treasure to Him.

You might be familiar with the story of the prodigal son. Jesus told this story about a man who had two sons. One wasn't very respectful and took his inheritance and moved away, while the second son stayed home and remained faithful to the father by doing his chores and everything else that was asked of him. The first son spent all his money and made very bad decisions, but he soon realized his mistakes and went back home to ask the father's forgiveness. The son's return home ended with a big celebration because the father never stopped loving his son. This is the same kind of love that Jesus has for you!

*Lord, I'm amazed You love me the same way God
loves You! Thank You. I will never truly understand it,
but I'm forever grateful for Your unfailing love.*

TAKE GOOD CARE

*"This is what I tell you to do: Love each
other just as I have loved you."*
JOHN 15:12

Jesus loves you with an indescribable love. He wants it to overflow from your heart to all the people around you. He wants this love to motivate you to take care of people and help them turn their eyes toward Jesus.

Being a good friend means helping others know they're important. It means listening to what they have to say. Sometimes life can get so busy that it's hard to stop and put other people first. But taking good care of your friends and family is a great way to show them the love of Jesus.

Jesus is proud of all the hard work you are doing, and He will continue to take care of you and provide everything you need. Stay connected to Him through His Word and prayer. You will help so many people when you let the love Jesus has for you spill into the lives of others.

*Jesus, please show me how to direct the love You
give me to all the people I come in contact with.
Help me serve them. I pray You get all the glory!*

THE ONE TO PRAISE

*My lips will praise You because Your
loving-kindness is better than life.*

PSALM 63:3

Jesus blesses you every day. You may not always feel it or see it, but it's true. He loves you and is in control of every part of your life. When you understand this truth and trust that He is the promise keeper, you will begin to spend more time praising Him.

When you don't have a "Jesus is in control" mindset, when you don't trust that Jesus will do what He says He will do, your heart becomes overwhelmed with worry and anxiety. The Bible includes many stories about people who began to worry about their situation and tried to handle it all on their own—but nothing ever worked out that way. They needed Jesus to handle it!

What you have with Jesus is better than anything you could ever have all on your own. His grace is what makes all things possible. Take time to thank Him and let your actions be your praise back to Him, because He is worthy!

*Lord, thank You for this new day. I want to make the
most of it by praising You. I can't thank You enough
for Your love. You are so wonderful to me!*

DO NOT FEAR

"Do not fear, for I am with you. Do not be afraid, for I am your God. I will give you strength, and for sure I will help you. Yes, I will hold you up with My right hand that is right and good."

Isaiah 41:10

Living as a child of the King means you have *nothing* to worry about. God promises to always have your back in every situation. He does this by guiding you with His Word, the Bible, and showing you how to make the best choices and be more like Jesus.

As you stay mindful of sharing the good news, don't forget that the Lord is with you and will help you accomplish things you never thought you could. Can you think of some ways to be a blessing to your family and friends? Be intentional in your relationships and practice putting others first. The more you think of others, the less time you'll have to worry about things.

Your actions say a lot about your heart! Your words will have more meaning when people see that Jesus has changed you from the inside. God made you special. Remember that today. Don't worry—God's got you!

Jesus, please forgive me when I worry. I know better, but sometimes I let my anxiety get the best of me. Show me how to rest in Your promises. Help me not to fear. Remind me that You are bigger than any problem I will ever face.

EVERY-MORNING MERCIES

It is because of the Lord's loving-kindness that we are not destroyed for His loving-pity never ends. It is new every morning. He is so very faithful.
LAMENTATIONS 3:22-23

Every day is a gift from God. God loves you so much that He wants you to enjoy every moment with Him. His kindness toward you will never end because He is forever faithful. He wants you to learn from Him and love like Him.

He loves you so much that He sent Jesus to make a way for you to be saved. He shows you His mercy every day. It's like the moon at night. You look up and see the moon's glow—which is really coming from the sun's rays—making this beautiful light in the darkness.

Jesus shines mercy on you every day, and you, in turn, shine like the moon and all the stars combined. Let this truth keep you confident and brave as you tell the world about your Savior, Jesus. He will not let you fail. You are doing great things because of Him. Keep looking for ways to be a blessing to others. Do the right thing even when it's hard and watch how Jesus opens more and more doors for sharing His love.

Lord, I'm so grateful You always show me mercy. I've messed up so many times, but You were always there to catch me. Thank You for the gift of today.

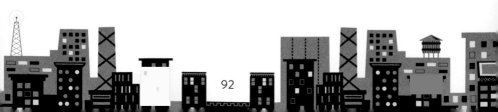

THE GREAT HEALER

He heals those who have a broken heart.
He heals their sorrows.
PSALM 147:3

Jesus loves to take care of you. He loves to lift you up when you feel sad. The Bible constantly shows us how He is the Healer. When He went to the cross, He healed us of our sins. When He saved you, He healed you from a life of darkness and shame. And when He set you on this world-changing adventure, He healed you from a life of selfishness—because your focus became all about making Him famous.

Pay close attention to all Jesus has done for you. Thinking about His goodness and grace will help you to become more like Him. Pray for the people you meet who are sad. Help your friends by listening when they tell you about the hard times they're going through. Putting others first will let them know they are important.

Living your life for Jesus is an awesome privilege. Encouraging people when they're down is a great way to practice being like Jesus. It shows others that you really care.

Thank You, Lord, for letting me be a part of Your
world-changing plan. Help me tell others about
You and Your ability to heal them from their sins.

HE IS WITH YOU

The Lord is with me. I will not be
afraid of what man can do to me.
PSALM 118:6

Understand with everything in your heart, mind, and soul that Jesus thinks you're special. He looks at you and is proud of who you are and what you're doing. He has promised that, with Him, we will have true peace in this life. Stay connected to His promises and never forget how much you mean to Him.

Jesus wants you to feel brave and courageous, knowing that nothing that can happen to you will take Him by surprise. That's why He tells you not to be afraid of anything, because He is always there by your side.

Think back over the last few days and consider your blessings. Can you see how Jesus wants to help you and comfort you? Whether you feel it or not, He's there and He'll never let go of you. He took all pain and suffering to the cross, where He made a way for you to be with Him—not only now but *forever*. Spend time today thanking Him for His great love for you!

Jesus, I love knowing You're right here with me. It helps
me not to worry. Please watch over me today and
lead me. In Your precious name I pray. Amen.

FULL OF KINDNESS

*The Lord is full of loving-pity and kindness. He is
slow to anger and has much loving-kindness.*

PSALM 103:8

The Lord is good. He is there to show you kindness all the time. He orchestrates events in your life that will show you just how much He cares about you. It's wonderful to think that the Creator of the universe, your heavenly Father, cares about you and wants to know everything that's on your heart.

If you haven't already, make it a daily habit to go to the Lord in prayer. When the Bible says Jesus has pity on you, that's not a bad thing. It just means He truly feels all the things you feel. Whether you're happy or sad, Jesus feels *all of it* with you.

Know that when you mess up, God isn't mad at you. His Spirit in you will prompt you to feel bad for messing up, because God wants you to learn from your mistakes. But He doesn't want you to sit and feel bad about yourself, because He loves you too much for that. Let your kindness and good deeds overflow from your heart to the world around you. That's a sure way to show people how much Jesus cares for them too!

*Jesus, I'm so glad that when You look at me You're proud and
that You show me kindness. I'm grateful You're not ashamed
of me. Please help me share Your kindness with others.*

FAITHFUL

"The Lord your God is God, the faithful God. He keeps
His promise and shows His loving-kindness to
those who love Him and keep His Laws."

DEUTERONOMY 7:9

God has so many awesome characteristics, there aren't enough books to list them all. One of His traits that brings you peace and comfort in the middle of every bad day is His faithfulness.

You can be certain that there will be days when you don't understand why things went the way they did. But that's okay, because God is faithful—and that means He is always with you and using you for good. His faithfulness means He's in control and that nothing happens without Him knowing about it. He will take all your uncertainty and worry and anxiety and turn them into good because of His faithfulness.

God wants you to spend time with Him every day. Quality time with Him will help you love Him and His Word more than anything else in your life. In your daily quiet time is where you will see His eternal faithfulness. This is where you will know how much He loves you. You will feel His goodness to you in the deepest part of your soul.

Jesus, I am so grateful that You care for me and that You
are always faithful. Please help me tell others about You.
Please help me know that even if I can't see it, You're
always at work and You always keep Your promises!

HIS GREAT LOVE

*And now we have these three: faith and hope
and love, but the greatest of these is love.*
1 CORINTHIANS 13:13

Open up your Bible, and you'll find example after example after example of how much God loves you. Let these examples encourage your heart as you go through this new day with God close by your side.

There's a great lesson in your Bible that Jesus wants you to remember. He reminds us that our first goal should be to love God with all our heart, mind, and soul. And the second part of the command is that we love our neighbors as we love ourselves. To love God first and then others is key when it comes to changing the world.

God's love warms your heart and fills you with a confidence that you can't get anywhere else. His love will guide you through all of life's storms. It is the only thing that will give you true peace on earth. Don't ever take His love for granted. It's the one thing that will never let you down.

*Dear Lord, thank You for Your love. Thank You for showing
me that I matter. Please help me rely on Your love for me.
I need it to overcome all my doubts and fears.*

GIVE YOUR LIFE

*We know what love is because Christ gave His life
for us. We should give our lives for our brothers.*
1 John 3:16

Jesus loves you so much that He came down from heaven to be born in lowly circumstances and to lead a humble life that ended on the cross. His love for you was so great that He gave up His life so your sins could be forgiven and you could spend forever with Him. Making the lives of others more important than your own is living as Jesus lived.

Your world-changing adventure won't always be easy, but it will always be rewarding. Knowing that you're making Jesus famous and sharing His love with the world is pretty amazing.

Start to see each new day as a gift from God. See each day as a fresh opportunity to give your life away for the sake of His good news and great love. What better prize than to see your friend or family member come to know Jesus in a personal way. You matter—and it can't be said enough just how much Jesus loves you. You bring Him so much joy. In return, He always wants you to stand right in the middle of His peace. Continue to be courageous and give your life so others may come to know the living God too!

*Lord, thank You so much for taking my place on the cross
so that all my sins could be forgiven. Help me to live an
unselfish life so people will see You when they see me.*

YOUR SAFE PLACE

Trust in Him at all times, O people. Pour out your heart before Him. God is a safe place for us.

PSALM 62:8

The Lord is always with you. He wants you to trust that He has a plan for your life. He is with you and will always take care of you, no matter what. He will never change the way He feels about you, and He will continually surround you with His unfailing love.

The Lord God is your safe place. With Him, you can be exactly who He made you to be. He wants you to tell Him everything and to know that He's not only listening to every word you say but also has the right answers to all your questions. The Lord loves you so much that He will show you He is thinking about you and meeting your needs in very specific ways. Just like a good earthly father, your heavenly Father loves to bring delight to His children!

Consider each one of your days from a new perspective. Grow with Jesus. Pour out your heart to Him. Begin to feel safe with Him. Your life is protected and filled with hope as you trust Him more and more.

Lord God, I can't live this life without You. I'm so thankful and happy that You are my one safe place. Thank You for being with me forever!

HE KNOWS YOUR NAME

"See, I have marked your names on My hands.
Your walls are always before Me."
ISAIAH 49:16

You are never alone. Jesus is always with you. The Bible says your name is written on God's hands. The one who made you not only loves you but has your name right there in front of Him forever. The same hands that were stretched out on Calvary's cross are the same hands that lovingly hold your name!

There will certainly be times when you don't feel the love of Jesus, but you need to understand that the truth is different from your feelings. You might feel scared, but the truth is that God is always with you—and He is bigger than any feelings or problems you will ever encounter in life.

Jesus wants you to feel calm and to live in the middle of His peace for you. His love is like a gentle breeze that brings relief on a warm day. The hope He gives will always make things better for you. Rely on His goodness and be confident as you tell people about His amazing gift of salvation.

Jesus, it's hard for me to understand that my name is written on Your hands. How amazing that my name is with You forever! I praise Your holy name!

GOOD MADE PERFECT

*And to all these things, you must add love. Love holds
everything and everybody together and makes
all these good things perfect.*
COLOSSIANS 3:14

It can't be said enough that Jesus is proud of all the hard work you are doing to make Him famous in your corner of the world. He wants to remind you to add love to everything you do. Love is *so important* to Jesus. It was the reason He came from heaven to take up His cross so that one day you could live with Him forever!

The Bible reminds us that real love from Jesus is like spiritual glue that holds all of God's children together. Love helps our lights continue to shine brightly in this dark world.

Love can take something good and turn it into something perfect, because that's just what Jesus does. With Him, you will always be loved, you will always be wanted, and you will always be cared for. Let all of these wonderful gifts from God overflow to the people you come in contact with so their eyes can turn to Jesus. Then they too will find that good things turn into perfect things—by His grace and love.

*Lord, help me rely on Your love more and more each day. I pray that
You will help me understand just how powerful Your love is so that
I won't be anxious or afraid of anything that comes my way.*

BE HAPPY

Be happy with what you have. God has said,
"I will never leave you or let you be alone."
HEBREWS 13:5

There are times when you might feel sad or anxious. Those feelings are normal sometimes. But as you walk each day with Jesus, He wants you to know that He will take care of you. He wants you to find the true happiness that comes from Him alone. He wants you to be content with all the things He has given you.

Jesus wants you to remember that He will never leave you. He is right there with you to fill your heart with His love and to remind you of the plans He has for your life. Part of those plans include sharing the gospel so the world will be changed for His glory.

Take some time to think about Jesus and His beautiful heart. Think about all the love He has for you. Let it warm your heart and calm your spirit. Feel true happiness rise from the joy He plants in your heart.

Lord, honestly, it's hard to feel happy a lot of the time. Things happen and I feel down and worried. Help me know Your truth. Help me receive the joy and happiness that come only from You.

LOVE EACH OTHER

Do not owe anyone anything, but love each other. Whoever loves his neighbor has done what the Law says to do.

ROMANS 13:8

The Bible mentions over and over again just how much God loves people. His love is unfailing. It's eternal. It's filled with hope. And when Jesus talked about the greatest of all the commands, He said that after you love the Lord with everything that's in you—heart, mind, and soul—you are to love your neighbor as you love yourself.

Usually when you owe somebody something, it's because you borrowed it. Maybe they had a cool book or toy, and you asked if you could borrow it for a while. When you're done with it, you give the item back. When Jesus talks about loving your neighbor, it's an "all give" situation. This means you give love without expecting anything in return.

As you work on sharing the gospel message, look to Jesus as a perfect example of giving in love and not taking anything out of selfishness. He loved His children so much that He died on the cross to forgive our sins. He literally gave up His life in love so that we would never be without Him. Praise His holy name forever!

Jesus, I can't thank You enough for sacrificing Your life because You loved me so much. Help me to love my family and friends as I tell them about You. I pray that Your love, overflowing from my heart, will help change the world for Your glory.

JUST LIKE JESUS

"I do not call you servants that I own anymore. A servant does not know what his owner is doing. I call you friends, because I have told you everything I have heard from My Father."

JOHN 15:15

Jesus is the best example of how we should treat one another. He loves us with an unconditional love. It's easy to care about people when everything is going well; but when life gets tough, loving others get a whole lot harder. But in Jesus we see how to treat others with kindness and respect no matter what. He loves when it's easy. He loves when it's difficult.

Every day you wake up is a chance to become more like Jesus. When you practice loving other people the way He loves you, then you care and serve without expecting anything in return. Whether it's doing your chores without being told or going out of your way to be kind and brighten your family's day, these kinds of actions share the love of Jesus and plant the seeds of hope in others.

Rejoice in the truth that Jesus loves you more than you will ever know. Receive His never-ending grace and feel His loving arms hold you close!

Dear Lord, I don't understand how You love me so much, but I'm so grateful You do. Help me extend that same love to my family and friends. Show me how to love like You love.

BIBLE STUDY

*Trust in the Lord with all your heart, and do
not trust in your own understanding.*
PROVERBS 3:5

Your Bible will be your most important resource as you begin sharing the love of Jesus with the world. So many encouraging verses and lessons are found in God's Word. You will be blessed beyond measure as you spend daily time reading your Bible.

Over and over again, God reminds His people that He always knows what's best for them. As humans who make a lot of mistakes, if we ignore God's commands, we set ourselves up for failure. When you make it a habit to read your Bible every day, you are, in a sense, planting God's wisdom in your mind, body, and soul. Scripture tells us that God's words are alive and active. Isaiah 55 even says His Word goes out and does a good work and then returns to Him after it has served its purposes.

Make a commitment to study your Bible. Then make time to listen to the Lord after you read His Word. You will soon see that trusting Jesus is *always* the best choice!

*Father God, I am so thankful for my Bible. I know there are many places
in the world where people don't have access to one. Please help me make
time for reading Your Word every day. I pray You'll teach me many things.*

ONE DAY

Dear friends, we are God's children now. But it has not yet been shown to us what we are going to be. We know that when He comes again, we will be like Him because we will see Him as He is.

1 JOHN 3:2

Not only has Jesus promised never to leave you alone, but He also promises that you will see Him face-to-face one day! Can you imagine? You will see Jesus, and He will hug you and tell you how much He loves you!

Jesus wants this good news to encourage you as you spend your days telling people about Him and His unfailing love. He wants you to look forward to that exciting day when all the pain and sadness and worry and anxiety of this world are erased forever. He wants you to eagerly await that moment when you are held in His arms and nothing else will matter.

It's hard to believe, but it's true. Jesus even told His friends that after He rose from the dead and went back to heaven, He would prepare a place for each one of us. And He also said that if He was doing all of that, He would come back for all His children so they could be with Him forever. So, child of the living King, be confident and courageous as you go about changing the world!

Lord Jesus, I cannot imagine what that day will be like when I get to see You and be hugged by You and hear You say You love me over and over and over again!

DON'T GIVE UP!

Live with love as Christ loved you. He gave Himself for us,
a gift on the altar to God which was as a sweet smell to God.
EPHESIANS 5:2

Your world-changing journey doesn't involve just telling people about all the things that Jesus has done for them; it also means living in such a way that your choices and actions become like a gift back to God. Your good living is like a gift of thanks to your Father in heaven for sending Jesus.

You know that God is proud of you and loves you immensely. Just as your parents are there to cheer you on, so is God. He loves you more than anyone else, and so He will be more excited about your accomplishments than anyone else ever could be.

When you live your life with love, you treat other people the way Jesus would treat them—with respect, dignity, kindness, and so much more. None of us is perfect—only Jesus—but that doesn't mean we can't try to be more and more like Him each and every day.

Lord, please help me to act like You. I know I'm going to make
a million mistakes, but I really want to try. Teach me and give
me a tender heart for the things that are important to You.

BEAUTIFUL DAY

May you have God's loving-favor.
TITUS 3:15

God made you very special. Out of the billions of people He has made, you are the only you. Think about that for a moment and then realize how important and unique and awesome you are. God has huge plans for your life. He doesn't want you to waste time worrying or being afraid, because you are loved and protected by the King of kings.

When you have a humble attitude and live to bring honor to Jesus, you are setting yourself up to receive God's loving favor. Think of it as God showering you with endless amounts of kindness and blessing. He knows what you need, and He is so good and faithful that you will always receive His best.

Be intentional today and make a decision that might be hard, yet you know in your heart it's the right decision to make. It's a decision that will make God proud and that may even show a friend that Jesus is your everything!

Thank You, Jesus, for Your favor. Thank You for looking at me and seeing someone special even when I can't. Thank You for believing in me even when I don't believe in myself.

YOUR DESIRE

*Be happy in the Lord. And He will
give you the desires of your heart.*
PSALM 37:4

When you think about your day, put God in the middle of it all. Make Him the center of your attention and the reason for everything you do. When you make God your first priority, you will find true happiness.

So many things happen each day that can make you feel like God is not in control. But when you make it a habit to put Him front and center, life's problems won't fill you with anxiety. Instead, the hard times will cause you to rely on God even more because you know He's faithful.

A man in the Old Testament named Job went through an unbelievable series of very bad days. He wondered what God was doing, but through it all he never stopped believing that God was good and that God was in control. Even when people told Job that God had forgotten about him, Job held on to hope that God was in charge. God eventually blessed Job even more than before all the problems started, and Job knew that God loved him with an unfailing love!

*Dear Father God, sometimes bad things happen and I feel anxious
and sad. Please teach me how to always rely on Your goodness
and love. Help me to remember that You want what's best for me
and that You're always in control. Thank You for loving me.*

ALL THINGS

We know that God makes all things work together for the good of those who love Him and are chosen to be a part of His plan.
ROMANS 8:28

Everything you experience today, God experiences too. That's because He is always with you, right there by your side. He will never leave you alone or turn His back on you. He will never roll His eyes or say that He doesn't like you. He made you special, and He makes everything come together for His good plan.

Even when things seem to be falling apart, hold on to hope! God has chosen you and calls you His precious child. He sees you and is so proud. He knows you'll go through hard times and carry heavy burdens, but through every single hardship, He is with you and will help you.

God is the promise maker and the promise keeper. He never promised that each of your days would be awesome, but He does promise that He will take care of everything and rewrite your story into something good. You are loved by the Creator. You are adored by the King! Nothing can bring you down low enough to be outside His reach. Close your eyes, take a deep breath, and exhale. Now open your eyes and know this: you matter!

Lord God, help me to understand that when I go through stressful times, it doesn't mean You have left me alone. Help me understand that You are always with me to uplift me and help me. Thank You for taking even the yucky things in life and making something good and wonderful from them.

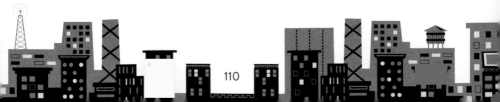

NEVER ALONE

Those who know Your name will put their trust in You. For You,
O Lord, have never left alone those who look for You.
PSALM 9:10

You mean the world to Jesus! He cares about you more than you will ever know. He doesn't want you to feel sad or alone. He doesn't want you to feel left out or unwanted. Instead, Jesus wants you to know that the world is a better place because you're in it. The people around you are better because they know you and are blessed by your friendship. You can change lives for the better just because you're you!

Another truth that is equally important for you to know is that you're never alone! Jesus is with you no matter where you go or what you're feeling. You may find yourself feeling scared or unsure. You might feel like you're in a situation where there is no answer and your prayers seem to have gone unanswered. The truth is that God can't ever leave you alone. You can trust Him because He doesn't lie. He means what He says, and He says that He will always be with you.

Take some time to think about these two crucial truths: you mean everything to Jesus and He never leaves you alone. You are very special to Him, and He won't ever let you forget it!

Jesus, I'm sorry I worry and wonder about my worth
to You. Some days I just feel like no one sees me and
that I'm alone. Remind me that You're right here!

FULL HEART

The Lord is my strength and my safe cover. My heart
trusts in Him, and I am helped. So my heart is
full of joy. I will thank Him with my song.

PSALM 28:7

It's important to remember that Jesus is the source of your strength. Many days you will feel tired and worn out, but Jesus is still at work in you and in the people around you. He promises to help you and give you what you need to be successful.

The Bible also says that you are safe with Jesus and that your heart should always trust in His goodness. Jesus wants you to know that He will help you—and not just in the big things, but in all the little things too. As you experience His loving care, your heart will be filled with joy, deep and lasting joy that comes from heaven.

You're probably familiar with the worship music at your church or on the radio. Professional musicians make it look easy. By putting all the chords together and singing all the right notes at the same time, they create a beautiful symphony of sound. In a similar way, your life lived for Jesus makes beautiful music lifted up to Him. Your life is a song of joy because He loves you!

Lord, I can't thank You enough for caring about everything I
go through. Thank You for being my safe place and the source
of my strength. Thank You for being with me forever.

KNOW HIM

Be quiet and know that I am God. I will be honored
among the nations. I will be honored in the earth.
PSALM 46:10

Life gets busy and overwhelming at times. It's easy to get wrapped up in daily drama and forget Jesus is right there with you. It's easy to forget that He's in charge and that He has everything you need.

The Bible tells us that God wants us to practice being quiet and still before Him so that we will know how awesome and mighty He really is. That's the key as you go about sharing His good news with others. The more time you spend sitting with Him in silence and thinking about His words for you in the Bible, the more your heart will become sensitive to the things that are important to Him. In turn, He will help you take that knowledge and wisdom out into the world as you share the good news.

If you already are spending daily quiet time with the Lord, praying, reading your Bible, and thinking about Him and the lessons He has for you, perfect! Keep it up! If not, start today! Have your breakfast and get ready for school, and then spend some time with God. You'll be amazed how each day gets better and better. God is so proud of you and the great things you will do for His glory.

I pray that You will help me have a better quiet time
with You, Jesus. Help me to rest quietly and listen for
Your guidance. Help me to grow closer to You, Lord.

YOUR HOPE

*Our hope comes from God. May He fill you with joy
and peace because of your trust in Him. May your hope
grow stronger by the power of the Holy Spirit.*
ROMANS 15:13

You've learned a lot of awesome truths about who God is and who He says you are! And while there are many more lessons to learn, it's a good time to take a minute to think about the goodness of God—specifically how good He is to you!

There are times in life when days are difficult and it seems like nothing ever goes the way you want it to. On days like these, putting your hope in Jesus is the only way to make it through. When you put your hope in Him, you trust that everything He says is true. The enemy wants us to believe that our Bibles are full of made-up stories written by people who lived long ago. When we have bad days, he wants us to believe that God must be off doing something else instead of caring for His children. But we know better, because God is so good!

Because we have hope that the Lord will never let us down, our hearts can always find joy in the middle of the hard days. As our faith grows, we rely on Jesus more and more—so our hope in Him grows too. Let His holy joy and peace fill your heart forever as you trust in Him.

*Lord, thank You for taking care of me all the time. Please keep
holding me close and leading me to the places You want me to go.*

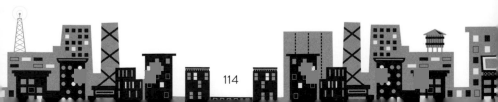

GOD'S GOT THIS

*"I tell you this: Do not worry about your life. Do not worry about
what you are going to eat and drink. Do not worry about
what you are going to wear. Is not life more important than
food? Is not the body more important than clothes?"*
MATTHEW 6:25

Jesus told His friends many times not to worry or be afraid about anything because He was in charge. The same is true for us today. Jesus doesn't want you worrying about anything because He is in control.

There was a specific time when Jesus told His friends not to worry about their lives because He was taking care of them just like He does for us today. He even pointed out that God feeds the birds, and even birds don't worry about where their next meal is coming from because of God's care for them. How much more does God care for you, brave boy?

Stop for a minute and think about the things that make you worry. Write them down and then share them with God. Ask Him to take your worries and replace them with His perfect peace. You'll be amazed at how different your days will be when you make it a habit to trust that God has you covered.

*Jesus, I'm sorry that I worry a lot. I forget that You're my
protector. Forgive me. Help me trust that You are in complete
control and that You will always give me everything I need.*

UNCHANGING

Jesus Christ is the same yesterday and today and forever.
HEBREWS 13:8

One of the great things about Jesus is that He never changes. As humans, we change our minds every day, every hour, sometimes by the minute. But with the Lord, it's different. He loved you yesterday more than you could ever imagine. He loves you today more than you could ever imagine—and tomorrow and every day after that He will continue to love you more than you will ever know.

This truth is reassuring because we never have to worry whether He cares for us or protects us or loves us—He never changes! He thought you were awesome yesterday, and He thinks you're awesome today! How does understanding this special characteristic of Jesus help you to be strong and courageous on your world-changing journey?

So many things in this world change, but Jesus never will. He will always be your Savior. He will always be your rock. He will always be your everything. Stay connected to Him forever, brave one, and let Him take care of you. He always wants what's best for you!

Jesus, thank You for never changing Your mind about me!
Please keep reminding me of Your love for me. I love You, Lord.

GOOD HOPE

*Good will come to the man who trusts in
the Lord, and whose hope is in the Lord.*
JEREMIAH 17:7

The Lord promises good things to His children who put their hope and trust in Him. To trust in Jesus means that no matter how you feel, you will obey His teachings because He holds the most important place in your life. There might be a time when you don't see a solution to a particular problem you're facing, but you believe that Jesus is *for* you and so you just take the next step.

Hope is the other part of receiving God's goodness. Hope means you expect certain things to happen. Normally when we deal with people, we're told not to have high expectations because people will let us down. But God wants us to hope for and expect His love and goodness. His mercy and grace for you will never run out!

The apostle Paul in the book of Acts is the perfect example of someone who trusted and kept his hope in Jesus. Paul faced so many difficult days and challenging circumstances, but he never stopped trusting and never stopped hoping in Jesus. His life made Jesus famous, and yours will too!

*Lord, no matter what happens in my life, I will trust that You know
what's best for me every time. Please help me keep hoping in You
and Your love for me. I know You are good every day of my life!*

STRONG TRUST

*He will not be afraid of bad news. His heart
is strong because he trusts in the Lord.*
PSALM 112:7

By now you should know that Jesus never changes. His love for you is unfailing and constant, which is why you can trust Him no matter what. He loves you whether you have a good day or a bad day, because He is always there and always in control.

The Bible says that God's children who trust in Him have strong hearts. This means that on bad days, they *still* have complete trust in Him. A strong heart will help you fully trust God's truth instead of your feelings. Your quest to change the world for God's glory depends on your decision to keep trusting Him and His promises for your life.

The Bible tells about a man named Matthew who is a good example of someone who had complete trust in Jesus. When he met the Lord for the first time, Matthew was nervous because he had been living a selfish life as a tax collector. But then a beautiful thing happened, and he decided to trust Jesus and live the rest of his life in obedience to Him. Matthew worked at keeping his heart strong.

*Jesus, help me put down my selfish desires so I
will be able to trust You more! Help me act like
Matthew and trust and follow You forever.*

THINKING OF HIM

*You will keep the man in perfect peace whose
mind is kept on You, because he trusts in You.*
ISAIAH 26:3

If you were to sit down and make a list of all the things you think about in a day, you might run out of paper. What would be on your list? Friends? Video games? Family? School? Pets? Our brains are active and always thinking about something. It's important that you spend time thinking about Jesus and His truth. One way to do this is to memorize a scripture from your Bible reading time and think about it throughout your day. Or maybe at church you could take notes on the pastor's sermon and then think about how you could apply that teaching during the week. . . .

The more time you spend in prayer and Bible reading, the easier it will be to think about the things of Jesus. Ask Him to reveal more of who He is so that you will have your mind connected to the things that really matter. Jesus promises to give you His peace and to fill your heart with His love. Now those are two awesome things you could think about all day long!

*Lord, I want to know all about You. I want to live my life in
a way that makes You proud. I want to tell people about You.
Help me keep my mind on You throughout each day of the week.*

AVOIDING TRAPS

*The fear of man brings a trap, but he
who trusts in the Lord will be honored.*
PROVERBS 29:25

When Jesus started His earthly ministry, the enemy came to try to tempt Him. You might remember the story. Satan was trying to get Jesus to become so self-centered that He'd forget the mission God had planned for Him. The devil made empty promises, but Jesus knew that His heavenly Father was in control and that the enemy was nothing but a liar.

The Bible tells us that if we live in fear of things and other people, we'll miss out on the blessings God has for us. But when we keep our trust in Jesus, the Bible says He will honor us. Trusting in Jesus to have all the answers is not always easy, but it is always the right thing to do.

Remember Adam and Eve? They messed up big-time. God was so good, however, that He didn't leave them in fear and shame. Instead, He offered a new life if they would trust His plans for them. They had to leave the paradise garden that He had originally given them, but in the end, they let go of fear and trusted their Creator!

*Lord Jesus, I want to trust You with everything in my
life. Please teach me to keep my focus on You and to
not worry about what other people say or think.*

TROUBLE-FREE

"Do not let your heart be troubled. You have put your trust in God, put your trust in Me also."
John 14:1

So many things can happen in life to take your mind off Jesus. Be aware when those times come, and pray that the Lord will keep your eyes focused on Him alone. Let His love fill your heart. Give Him your worries and fears.

Jesus wants you to trust Him because He is your perfect Savior who loves you and has an amazing plan for your life. He doesn't want to see you sad or upset, and He certainly doesn't want you to feel shame. So, brave boy, the best thing for you to do is to put your trust in His Word.

Do you remember the story about Jonah and the whale from Sunday school? When God first called Jonah, the prophet's heart was troubled because he didn't want any part of obeying God. God told Jonah to preach in the city of Nineveh, but instead, Jonah ran away. He got on a boat and tried to travel in the opposite direction. And soon after, Jonah was swallowed by a huge fish! It took a while, but Jonah soon realized that God cared for him so much that He not only rescued him from the fish but taught him how to be obedient even in the tough times. God wants the same for you!

Jesus, I'm sorry for all the times I act like I don't need You. Please forgive me. Help me see that You are always with me. Help me trust You in every situation!

NO WORRIES

When I am afraid, I will trust in You.
PSALM 56:3

When you start to worry, ask Jesus for help. He knows your heart, and He knows that you want to change the world for His glory. He knows you want to tell as many people as possible about His loving-kindness. The bottom line is, Jesus is proud of you!

Usually when everything is going right, we rely on ourselves rather than Jesus. We might selfishly, and foolishly, think it's our good decisions that led to our success; but in reality, everything we have and everything we will become is because of Jesus.

Moses helped lead the Israelites out of Egypt to the promised land, but his journey wasn't easy. He was nervous to talk in front of the pharaoh, but God had already gone before him and made a way. And just as God parted the Red Sea for His children to cross safely, He is also making a way for you.

Believe that Jesus is always looking out for you. Know that He is always protecting you. Keep on trusting Him. He will never let you down, and He will always remove your fears.

Lord, thank You for the example of Moses. Help me to be like him and trust in Your perfect plan for my life. Help me to trust You so much that I never become fearful or worried about all the things that could happen to me. I love You, Jesus.

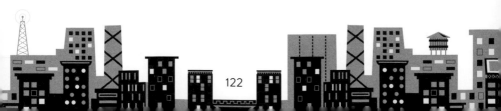

BETTER IS THE LORD

It is better to trust in the Lord than to trust in man.
PSALM 118:8

Life is full of choices. You know that just from going to the grocery store with your parents. There are a hundred different kinds of *everything* it seems, and it's all packaged to get your attention. There are things we need, things we don't need, and things we wish we had but can't afford. The list goes on and on. This is the way of our world, with so many things trying to compete for our attention.

Psalm 118 reminds us that as we go through life, we need to keep our eyes and hearts focused completely on the Lord. Check every decision with Him in prayer and spend time throughout the day thanking Him for every blessing He has given you.

This is where faith comes in. Since we can't see Jesus, our hearts must beat by faith. We must trust God instead of all the things our eyes see in the world around us. People might act like they have all the answers, but they don't. Rely on Jesus. Let Him guide your life. Let Him carry you and your burdens. He loves you more than you could ever know!

Jesus, thank You for leading me. Please help me stay connected to Your truth. Please keep holding me and loving me and letting me know that everything will be okay.

A GOOD PLACE

The Lord is good, a safe place in times of trouble.
And He knows those who come to Him to be safe.
NAHUM 1:7

Want to know something really cool? Jesus knows your name! Just like the day He called you to be His child forever, this new day that He is giving you is no different. He's calling you out of selfishness to do good work for His holy name. He's calling you from a place of uncertainty to one of confidence and courage.

You're never too young to share the gospel. You don't need a college degree to be qualified to tell people how amazing Jesus is. Right now, at the age you are, Jesus has given you everything you need to be bold and go out and change your world. Jesus is never taken by surprise or caught off guard like we are. You are safe with Him always, because He is good and always will be.

One way to change your world is by praising the Lord. Praise doesn't have to look like singing songs at church. Instead, it could be speaking about Jesus in your conversations with friends and teachers and family members. It's easier than you think. Since you're safe with Jesus and have the power of His Holy Spirit in you, you are capable of so much more than you could ever imagine!

Jesus, please show me how to praise You. Whether it's
through my words or actions, help me show other
people how much You mean to me.

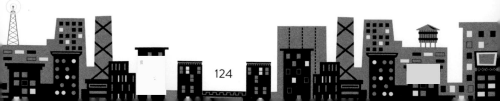

124

TAKEN CARE OF

Trust in the Lord, and do good.
So you will live in the land and will be fed.
PSALM 37:3

Today, remember that Jesus is taking care of you. He asks you to trust Him and obey His commands, because He knows what's best for you. How will this knowledge help you live a more courageous life?

There will be days when you don't feel like you can change one little thing, let alone the whole world. Don't let your feelings get in the way of all the good things Jesus has for you. Just trust that He is leading you and loving you. He will never abandon you or leave you to figure things out on your own. Jesus will always help you solve your problems. All you have to do is believe in Him and trust that He is in charge.

And never forget that your worth is in Him. This means you are free to be the person He created you to be. You matter to Him—always. You don't have to worry about doing enough good things to make Him happy. Just trust Him and follow where He leads. He will never let you down!

Lord, I'm sorry when I forget that You will always take
care of me. Help me rely on Your goodness all day long!

THE NAME

Some trust in wagons and some in horses. But we
will trust in the name of the Lord, our God.
PSALM 20:7

There's a constant temptation in life to put your trust in the things you can see and the things you can buy. Take your parents' car for example. The car helps you and your family go wherever you want, and it makes life so much easier. The car is something that is easily taken for granted—that is, until it breaks down.

If we're not careful, life can be like that car. From our comfortable home to our clothes and shoes. . .all that "stuff" is great, but if we forget who ultimately has provided those things for us, we miss the whole point.

Jesus is our provider. The car, the house, the clothes—all of those things break down or wear out at some point. But we've already learned that Jesus never changes. He never stops taking care of His children. That's why keeping your trust in Jesus and thanking Him for every blessing He ever gives is the best way to stay connected to your Lord and Savior. He is your constant source of hope!

Jesus, I'm sorry when I forget that my trust belongs
in You alone. Sometimes I get wrapped up in all the
"stuff" and forget that You're the one in charge.

GIVE HIM EVERYTHING

Trust in Him at all times, O people. Pour out your heart before Him. God is a safe place for us.

Jesus really wants to know how you're doing. He knows, of course, but He wants to have such a close relationship with you that you pour out your heart to Him all the time. He doesn't want you to hold anything inside or worry that you're bothering Him.

He wants you to trust Him with everything so that there's never a time when you wonder if He cares about you or is helping you. Share everything with Him. Don't hold anything back. Jesus wants to hear it all, because He's your safe place. You can tell Him anything and know that He's not judging you or ashamed of you. He loves you unconditionally and wants to help you with whatever you're going through.

You are important to the Lord, and He wants you to remember how special you are to Him. That's why He longs for you to tell Him anything and everything. He holds your life in the palm of His hand, so make Him the first one you run to with your hopes and dreams, your pain and sorrow, your worries and fears, and your joys and victories.

Jesus, thank You for being my safe place and caring about me more than anyone else does. Thank You for listening to everything I have to tell You. Thank You for being my King and being in charge of my life. Thank You for Your unfailing love!

MORNING, NOON, AND NIGHT

Let me hear Your loving-kindness in the morning, for I trust in You. Teach me the way I should go for I lift up my soul to You.
PSALM 143:8

Each morning the Lord gives you is a gift. Not only does He look over you while you sleep, but He's there to greet you with His love and care at the beginning of each new day. Just as the sun rises to brighten the morning sky, Jesus shines His light over you so that you will be taken care of. Notice the verb *hear* in today's scripture verse in regard to God's loving-kindness. Think of the birds singing in the early morning—even His creation lets you know that you are surrounded by His unfailing love.

As the hours pass and the sun climbs high in the sky to warm the land, Jesus is there to warm your heart. He wants you to trust Him and learn from His Word. Your world-changing journey will be filled with grace and hope as you follow your Savior. Keep your eyes on Him and your soul lifted toward heaven in eager anticipation of all He has planned for you.

At the end of a busy day, when nighttime arrives, the beautiful stars begin to appear in the sky. They sparkle like gems, just as your life shines in this dark and broken world. You are loved!

Thank You, Jesus, for filling my heart with Your unfailing love. I pray that it overflows to the world and lets others know who You are!

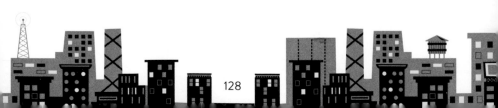

DON'T WORRY

I praise the Word of God. I have put my trust in God.
I will not be afraid. What can only a man do to me?
PSALM 56:4

The Bible is full of examples of the Lord telling His people not to worry. Jesus is in control of your life, and He listens to you because you're His. No one in the world will ever love you like He does!

Nothing can happen to you today that Jesus isn't a part of. Whether it's a ton of good things or a load of stressful stuff, Jesus doesn't want you to be afraid, because He's bigger than all of it put together. Focusing on His goodness and unfailing love helps you walk through this new day with confidence, knowing He is your promise keeper. He will always make a way even when life seems to be at a dead end.

Is there something on your heart that feels like it's too big even for Jesus? If so, know without a doubt that Jesus is fighting for you. He wants you to feel His love and protection. Hear Him call you brave, confident, and strong. Even if you don't feel all those things, the truth is that you are, because Jesus says so. Don't worry. Instead, worship Him!

Thank You for reminding me not to worry, Lord. I pray that I would trust You instead of being afraid. Please let me know You're here today, and help me to be more like You so I can continue to change my world.

MASTER PLAN

Trust your work to the Lord, and your plans will work out well.
PROVERBS 16:3

A lot of work goes into building a new house. A lot of people with a lot of different jobs come together to create the finished product—the architect and the engineer, the designer and the construction crew, the electrician and plumber and painter. Everyone's job is important. But without the blueprints, the house won't turn out right.

Your life has a plan for it too—a plan created by the Master. The one who made you and cares for you came up with a plan for your life because you matter, and He wants you to be a part of building His kingdom by sharing the gospel. He loves watching you follow His lead.

The man named Paul in the New Testament is a great example of someone whose life revealed the amazing providence of God's plan. Paul was a very powerful man who made a lot of bad decisions—and then one day, he met Jesus. Jesus turned his life upside down and gave him a new purpose. Part of the plan was hard and other parts were easy to live out, but all of them came together to serve a purpose. Jesus used Paul to change the world! Pray today and ask Jesus to show you more of His plan for your life. Follow Him boldly. You've got this!

Thank You, Jesus, for making a perfect plan for my life. Help me to be obedient so I can know You're here taking care of everything. Thank You for guiding me today!

THE GOOD LIFE

"I came so they might have life, a great full life."
JOHN 10:10

There are a lot of things that people buy to help them feel happy. Clothes, cars, video games, toys, books, vacations. . . The list goes on and on. But Jesus has a different answer for happiness.

He says that He is the answer—the *only* answer—to a full life. True joy and peace, hope and love, are found in Jesus alone. The Israelites experienced this truth firsthand when God rescued them from the clutches of Egypt and the pharaoh. It wasn't long before the people started complaining about life in the desert. Some of the Israelites even wished they could go back into slavery. A lot of them quickly forgot about God and started worshipping a golden calf statue. They were trying to find happiness in all the wrong places.

Think about all the things Jesus does for you, and you'll be reminded that the good life is found only in Him. Think about all the times you felt sad and then had a friend speak a kind word or a family member give you a hug. That kind of encouragement is from Jesus! As you go through today thinking of ways to make Jesus famous, remember that He is true joy.

Lord, I admit I try to find happiness in a lot of different things. But there always comes a time when the good feelings run out and I'm wondering what the next thing will be. Jesus, I know that You alone are my joy. Thank You for the good life You've given me.

SAFE AND SOUND

God is our safe place and our strength. He is always our help when we are in trouble.

PSALM 46:1

Each day is an opportunity for you to change your world by making good choices that honor the Lord. And that's great news! The problem, though, is that each day also brings with it the possibility of worry and fear. The enemy doesn't want you using your gifts and skills to make Jesus famous. He wants you to waste your time. He wants you to be overwhelmed with anxiety. But God is our help all the time. He can help us conquer the enemy.

What is one small thing you could do for someone else today? When you help other people, you are showing them that they matter. Your act of kindness tells them they are cared for and valued, and it plants the seeds of hope in their lives.

Jesus changed His world one person at a time. He was intentional with the people closest to Him, but He was also very much aware of the needs of strangers. Even though we're not Jesus, He calls us to serve and to extend grace and mercy just like He did. He calls us to be peacemakers and to live with humble hearts. When you make this your daily goal, you are helping people know that Jesus is their safe place and their eternal hope.

Lord, sometimes it's hard to think about other people when I feel like I'm dealing with so much myself. Help me to be like You by treating others with respect. Help me daily to become more like You and ultimately change the world for Your glory!

THE ONE WHO SAVES

*"See, God saves me. I will trust and not be afraid.
For the Lord God is my strength and song. And He
has become the One Who saves me."*

Isaiah 12:2

Many things will happen to you today that might make you feel happy or anxious or grateful. Whatever the case, make sure you stay connected to your Bible reading so that you will be able to separate truth from feeling. It's easy to get lost in your feelings and forget the truth that God is there with you to encourage and care for your heart.

God is always one step ahead, showing you the way He wants you to go. He saved you the moment you put your trust in Jesus, and He continues to be the one who saves you from hopelessness and despair. All He asks is that you trust Him so that fear will no longer be an issue. His love for you is stronger than anything else in the world.

Spend some extra time today thinking about the Lord not only as Your source of strength but as Your focus of worship. Your daily plans should always include praise to Jesus. Telling people about His love is like singing a song that celebrates the wonders of the King of kings.

*Thank You, Jesus, for this new day. Help me trust
You more. Remind me that You are always here to
encourage me and show me what's best for my life!*

THROUGH THE FIRE

When you pass through the waters, I will be with you. When you pass through the rivers, they will not flow over you. When you walk through the fire, you will not be burned. The fire will not destroy you.

Isaiah 43:2

God promises time and time again to be with you forever. He specifically says that when you pass through the hard times of life, He will keep you from being overwhelmed.

When the stressful times rise like a flood, they won't wash you away. When fear burns hot, God promises to keep it from destroying you. The hard times and anxiety do not define you. They may get in your way, and they probably don't feel very good, but the truth is that Jesus and His power help you push back against fear and sadness.

Your world-changing adventure should focus on sharing God's love with others. But it also should make you more confident of your place in the Lord's kingdom. God didn't make a single mistake when He breathed life into you, and He certainly won't make any mistakes as He guides you on your journey. Stay connected to His perfect plans for your life, and believe that He who calmed the raging sea is also powerful enough to calm the floods and fires that may cross your path.

Thank You, Jesus, for reminding me that You are greater than anything in the world. Thank You for telling me time and time again that You are bigger than my biggest problem. I praise Your name forever!

ASK

*We are sure that if we ask anything that
He wants us to have, He will hear us.*
1 JOHN 5:14

Before you go on a trip, you pack your clothes and other things you will need while you're away from home. If you find later that you forgot to pack something, you stop at a store and buy what you need. Either way, you make sure you have what's needed for your journey. But the Bible records a time when Jesus told His friends to pack nothing for their trip. He said He would make sure they had what they needed and assured them that people would feed them and take care of them along the way. Jesus didn't want His friends to be distracted by any of their stuff.

God is not like a cosmic vending machine where you ask for a million dollars and money starts falling from the sky. But He is your Father, and He will provide everything you need. Remember that you're never bothering Him. When you ask Him for help, He's there with encouragement and wisdom. Don't be afraid to ask for His blessing and provision. He loves to take care of you!

*Lord Jesus, I don't want to waste Your time or mine asking for
things I don't need. I do want to ask for wisdom so that I can
learn more about You each and every day. Thank You!*

LIVE BY FAITH

*Our life is lived by faith. We do not
live by what we see in front of us.*

2 Corinthians 5:7

Faith is a word that is used a lot when it comes to Jesus, but it might be hard to understand what it means. Faith is believing that God is who He says He is, even though you can't see Him. Faith is trusting that God is good and willing to help you through all of life's ups and downs.

Noah had faith. When God told him to build the ark, the Bible says that Noah was the only righteous person around. He probably wondered why the Lord was asking him to build a boat, yet he still did it. That's faith. Rahab also had faith. She lived in Jericho and helped the two Israelite spies, Joshua and Caleb. In turn, her life was spared when the walls crumbled and fell.

You have faith too. You've been spending each day with the Lord, thinking about His plans for your life. You've been praying and discovering ways to change your world. And even though you can't see Jesus, you know He's there. You've come to rely on His goodness through faith. Don't put your faith in anything else. Other things will let you down, but Jesus never will!

*Lord, please give me strength to keep my trust in You
and not in other things. Help me keep living by faith.
Thank You for everything You provide for me!*

MORE IMPORTANT

*"Look at the birds in the sky. They do not plant seeds.
They do not gather grain. They do not put grain into a
building to keep. Yet your Father in heaven feeds them!
Are you not more important than the birds?"*
MATTHEW 6:26

Jesus wants you to know how important you are to Him. This is such an important truth all throughout the Bible. You will find, time and time again, examples of how great His love is for His children and the lengths to which He'll go to save them.

Consider, for example, the very first story in the Bible about the Garden of Eden. You're probably very familiar with the gigantic mistake that Adam and Eve made when they disobeyed God and ate the fruit from the one tree God told them not to. Afterward, they felt full of shame and regret.

But God pursued Adam and Eve and reached out to them in love. He came up with a way to save them when they couldn't save themselves. He did it because He cared so much about them, just like He cares so much about you. The Bible reminds us that out of all His creation, His children are more important than any other part of it. In His eyes, you are valued, you matter, and He will take care of you beyond anything you can imagine!

*Thank You for taking care of me, Lord. Thank You for
loving me and calling me Your child. Thank You for
providing for me. Please help me not to worry.*

GOOD TO GO

When I am afraid, I will trust in You. I praise the Word of God. I have put my trust in God. I will not be afraid. What can only a man do to me?
PSALM 56:3–4

Maybe you've had to do a group project for school—one where everybody has a part to play in the final product. When everybody has done their work and the time has come to present it, the group can say, "We're good to go!" As you showcase your hard work, you might feel a little nervous because you don't like talking in front of people, but you are confident because you know you've done a good job preparing.

Doing your daily Bible study is one of the best ways you can prepare for each day of your world-changing adventure. Spending time in God's Word helps you trust Him more and more. God will always bless the time you spend with Him, and you will become braver and more confident as you walk with Him through each new day.

As you go about your daily routine, remember that you have nothing to be afraid of. Plan to make the most of every opportunity that comes your way. Be bold. Look for chances to share what Jesus has done for you. God is using you to help people realize that they matter to Him and are loved by Him. Be intentional with your conversations and spend time praying for your friends and family. You've got this! With God on your side, you're good to go!

Lord, I want to live boldly and with confidence because I know You are always with me. Forgive me when I worry. Help me remember You are in control!

UNCHANGING

"For I, the Lord, do not change. So you,
O children of Jacob, are not destroyed."
MALACHI 3:6

Some days you might feel that all your hard work isn't doing a single thing to change the world. But the Lord wants you to know the truth of the matter: He is using everything you do for good—even the little things!

The enemy wants you to feel defeated and alone. He wants you to be too busy to spend time in God's Word. He wants you to feel anxious when things don't go the way you planned. As a matter of fact, Satan tried tempting Jesus in similar ways. He wanted Jesus to use His power in selfish ways. He tried to get Jesus to bow down to him—to disconnect Jesus from His heavenly Father. But Jesus didn't want to have any part in the enemy's games. He quoted Bible verses back to Satan after each temptation. He stood strong on the truth that never changes.

No matter what you're facing today, know that Jesus understands. Since His love for you never changes, He will never let you be defeated. Instead of allowing feelings of helplessness into your heart, remain hopeful—because Jesus is carrying you through every hour of every day.

Lord God, some days are hard. And sometimes I don't understand what Your plan is for me. Show me how to take what I read in Your Word and apply it to my life. Thank You for always being the same awesome Savior!

WATCHING OVER YOU

He will not let your feet go out from under you.
He Who watches over you will not sleep.

PSALM 121:3

Did you know that God never sleeps and is always watching over you? He is so much bigger than we could ever imagine, but He is close enough to be where you are—all the time. You are His precious child, and you are worth so much to Him.

Jesus had a friend named Peter who was one of His apostles. They traveled everywhere together. Peter watched Jesus minister to people and perform miracles. Peter knew that Jesus was the Messiah and was grateful to spend so much time with Jesus. Fast-forward to the week that Jesus was crucified, and you might remember the story of Peter denying that he knew Jesus—not once, but three times!

Jesus was watching over Peter, even in that moment of extreme weakness. After Jesus rose from the dead and came back to spend time with His friends, He talked to Peter and put him in charge of the early church. Just like Peter, you can find peace and comfort in the fact that even when you make mistakes, Jesus will take care of you—and He will also use you to change the world!

Lord, I'm so grateful You are always watching over me.
And even though You're so big and mighty and I'm so
small and weak, You give me everything I need.

ABOVE ALL THINGS

But as for me, I trust in You, O Lord. I say, "You are my God."
PSALM 31:14

You might have heard the phrase "Go all in" or "Give 110 percent." Both phrases refer to putting all your effort into a job or activity or sport. It's the same as saying, "Don't hold anything back" when you're encouraging someone to put their mind to something.

When we live "all in" for God, we practice acting like Jesus no matter where we are or what we're doing. The Bible says that we are to love the Lord with our heart, mind, soul, and strength. That means *all of us, all in for His glory, all the time*. Because we're human, we'll probably make plenty of mistakes, but that shouldn't keep us from always trying to do our best.

Consider whether there are any areas of your life where you are not giving your all. Is there some selfish part of your life that you like to hang on to because it's comfortable and feels good? For example, do you like to come home from school and play video games instead of doing your homework? It's okay to play the games, but it's not okay to let your schoolwork suffer when the Lord has given you an awesome brain to be the best student you can be. If you think of areas in your life where you could be more diligent, ask the Lord to reveal ways you can go "all in" for Him. You will be so happy you did!

Jesus, please forgive me for the times I don't give my all to You. Forgive me for the times I'm selfish and act like I know better. Thank You for always helping me despite my weaknesses.

JOY-FILLED HEARTS

*But I have trusted in Your loving-kindness. My heart
will be full of joy because You will save me.*

PSALM 13:5

Being a world changer means that you are sold out for Jesus. You trust Him with everything in your life, and you make choices that bring Him glory. You are *all in, all the time*. Believing that God loves you and that He is good no matter what allows your heart to be filled with His joy.

The joy that Jesus gives is one that never lets you down. It brings a peace that comes from knowing He is the promise keeper who fights for you every hour of every day. The joy that Jesus gives also helps you look beyond the problems of life to that glorious day when struggles and pain are a thing of the past, and what lies ahead is an eternity of time with Jesus.

Jesus is our perfect example of how this joy works itself out in a person's life. Any problem He faced was a chance to show love and peace. When He calmed the stormy sea, He took His disciples' fear and gave them joy in return. When He went to the cross, He took the mocking and scorn and gave us eternal life. That's a joy that no one here on earth can comprehend!

*Lord, I need the joy You have for me each and every day. Help
me obey Your commands and trust You so that I can always
have a heart filled with Your peace and goodness.*

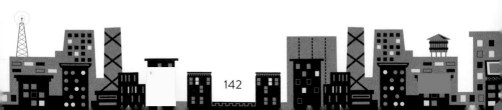

GREAT HOPE

Those who trust in the Lord are like Mount Zion,
which cannot be moved but stands forever.
PSALM 125:1

The enemy doesn't want you telling people about Jesus. He also doesn't want you living your life to honor God. Instead, he wants you to make decisions that are selfish and don't consider other people's feelings. The enemy knows you have Jesus in your heart, but that doesn't stop him from trying to lie to you.

The Bible calls the devil the father of lies. From the very beginning, he tried to find a way to make God's children feel unwanted and alone. When he tempted Adam and Eve to eat the fruit of the tree that was off-limits to them in the Garden of Eden, he was trying to get them to do their own thing. He wanted them to make their own decisions and not obey what God said. In the end, God took care of Adam and Eve, but they learned a hard lesson.

The Bible gives us great hope when we put our trust in Jesus. And the more we trust Jesus, the more we grow up into strong people who are like mountains that will never crumble and never be moved. Keep trusting Jesus more and more. He's doing a great work in you and will never stop protecting you.

Lord, I can't thank You enough for teaching me that
I can avoid the devil's lies by trusting You. Thank You
for building me up and never letting me down!

NEAR TO YOU

The Lord is near to all who call on Him,
to all who call on Him in truth.
PSALM 145:18

Aren't you comforted knowing that Jesus is with you all the time? He's bigger than your feelings and your current situation. He's better than the best day you've ever had, and He loves you more than anyone else ever will. He wants you to constantly call on Him and stay connected to His promises.

There's a great story in your Bible in the Gospel of John where Jesus meets a lady at a well. The lady had made a lot of bad decisions and she was ashamed. Jesus cared so much about her that He stopped and told her about His offer of living water. He was saying that a relationship with Him means that He is always with us and we'll never want for anything again.

The woman finally realized who Jesus was, and she surrendered her life to Him. Jesus used her in mighty ways. She returned to her village and told everyone she met about His love and kindness. Many people believed in Jesus because of her boldness and bravery. Jesus exchanged her sadness and shame for something miraculous.

Lord, I feel ashamed when I think about my sins and
mistakes. I'm so grateful that You have forgiven me
and that You still choose me to help change the world.

SURROUNDED BY LOVE

Many are the sorrows of the sinful. But loving-kindness will be all around the man who trusts in the Lord.

PSALM 32:10

Life isn't always wonderful. There are days when everything feels wrong, God seems far away, and you just don't know why things happen the way they do. Those are exactly the kinds of situations where Jesus loves to meet you and show you just how much He's taking care of you and surrounding you with His everlasting love.

Your world-changing journey will be filled with ups and downs, but the awesome thing is that Jesus holds you close every step of the way. The bad days don't define you and the good days can't compare to the joy Jesus gives you as you continue to trust and obey Him.

The Bible says that His love for you remains today and forever. You are in the middle of His unfailing, unending compassion. Let that truth sink in. Be confident that you are special because He says so. Be confident that you are worthy because He says you are. No matter what, always remember that God goes before you and protects you. Rejoice that He calls you His child. Celebrate the truth that you've been saved—forever!

Thank You, Jesus, for everything You do for me. Thank You for surrounding me with Your love and calling me Your precious child. Help me be more like You every day. I want to follow You everywhere You lead.

TO THE END

*"Teach them to do all the things I have told you. And I am
with you always, even to the end of the world."*
MATTHEW 28:20

Jesus not only is with you but has asked you to spread His story everywhere. He promises to guard you and guide you along the way as you share His truth with others.

Jesus doesn't want you to worry or feel like you are unqualified to be a world changer. When He created you, He gave you a special set of skills and talents that He didn't give anyone else. To be prepared to share the good news, continue reading His Word and strengthening your connection to His truth.

Moses helped set the Israelites free, but at first he thought he wasn't qualified for the job. You might know how the story ends. Moses eventually confronted the pharaoh multiple times. God helped Moses and the Israelites by sending ten plagues. . .and by the time all was said and done, the Israelites were out of Egypt and on their way to the promised land. Moses received his courage from the Lord and was able to stand up to the pharaoh. God kept His promise and freed His people. He will do the same thing through you as you obey Him in faith.

*Jesus, thank You for letting me be a part of sharing Your love with the
world and freeing people from their sin and shame. I'm grateful You're
always with me—I can't do any of Your world-changing work on my own!*

IN ALL THINGS

*He asks God to help you to be strong and to make
you perfect. He prays that you will know what
God wants you to do in all things.*

COLOSSIANS 4:12

God doesn't just want a relationship with you on Sundays. He wants you to connect with Him every day of the week, all day long. He wants you to rely on Him in every situation. He wants you to have confidence and become more like Jesus every day.

Jesus is a perfect example. He always wanted to do His Father's will. He stayed connected to God through quiet time and prayer. In times of suffering and in times of victory, no matter what His emotions were like, He knew His priority would always be to do what God wanted.

The book of Acts tells of a man named Ananias. The Lord commanded this man to help Paul right after he had the encounter with Jesus on the road to Damascus. Ananias knew Paul had been doing bad things to Christians, and he couldn't believe he was being asked to help such a bad person. But God explained to him that Paul's life was a new creation in Jesus. So despite his hesitation, Ananias obeyed God and took care of Paul so that Paul could begin his own world-changing journey.

*Lord, I want to do all the things You command me to
do so that I will bring You glory. Please help me,
especially when doing the right thing is hard.*

DO YOUR BEST

*Because of this, we work hard and do our best because
our hope is in the living God, the One Who would
save all men. He saves those who believe in Him.*
1 TIMOTHY 4:10

As a believer, you should always work hard—whether you're doing homework or chores around your house. When you work hard, you are creating opportunities to change your world, because people will notice your good attitude and see that you really care about all the things you are asked to do.

Nothing that God asks of you is ever a waste of time. People are always watching. They may never say something to you personally, but those who notice will wonder how and why you always have such a great attitude and enthusiastic work ethic. And when the opportunity presents itself, you will be able to tell them that it's all because of Jesus.

In the Gospel of Mark, people were bringing their sick friends and family to the center of a particular town so Jesus could heal them. The people even asked Jesus if they could touch the bottom of His coat—and those who did were healed. Behave in such a way that people begin to ask you questions. Then they can learn about Jesus so that ultimately they can be set free from their sin and look forward to spending forever with Him.

*Father God, I'm so grateful You saved me. Help me
work hard at everything I do. Help me have a great
attitude so I have chances to tell people about You!*

LIVING WATER

Jesus said to her, "You do not know what God has to give. You do not know Who said to you, 'Give Me a drink.' If you knew, you would have asked Him. He would have given you living water."
JOHN 4:10

When you meet with Jesus for the very first time, your world turns upside down. Regular water, as you know, quenches thirst. But eventually we become thirsty again. Living water, from Jesus, quenches your spiritual thirst forever.

It's easy to get caught up in prideful, selfish feelings. It's easy to believe you only need Jesus on the hard days. But the truth is, staying connected to Jesus allows you to receive His blessings. It also helps you to form a habit of relying on Him.

How can you make today different—and better—than yesterday? How can you rely on Jesus more? What will you do differently as you feel the rush of His living water pour over every aspect of your life? Will you pray for a friend? Will you help a neighbor? Will you tell someone about Jesus? Can you find a way to do something for someone else without expecting anything in return? These kinds of things will make the Lord's living water overflow from your heart to the world around you and ultimately change it for His glory!

Jesus, I pray that Your living water would flow through me and onto the people You bring into my life.

THINK ABOUT IT!

*But Mary hid all these words in her heart.
She thought about them much.*

LUKE 2:19

The words Mary had in her heart were the words of the shepherds who shared what an angel had told them about the baby Jesus. The angel had informed them that the baby was Christ the Lord and was the one who had come to save people from their sins. When the shepherds arrived at the place where Mary and Joseph were staying and saw the baby lying in the feeding trough, they knew He was Jesus!

Mary thought about what the shepherds said, and she thought about it often. Each one of us should continually remember that we belong to Jesus and that He is Christ the Lord! He isn't just somebody we pray to and worship on Sundays. He's so much more. In fact, we will never completely understand just how amazing and awesome He is until we get to see Him face-to-face one day.

Jesus is love. He is kindness and goodness. He is your protector and your help. He's your hope and your light and your great Shepherd who is always there for you. Today, as you wait to see how Jesus shows up for you, try having the same level of excitement and expectation as the shepherds. Plan on meeting Jesus today with eagerness and joy.

*Lord, help me think about You all the time. Help me
be as excited as the shepherds were that night You
were born. Help me wait eagerly for You today.*

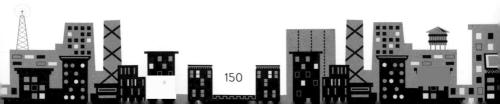

MAKE MORE FRUIT

"He takes away any branch in Me that does not give fruit. Any branch that gives fruit, He cuts it back so it will give more fruit."
JOHN 15:2

You might have seen a plant that looked like it was dying. No amount of water would ever be able to help. And then you might have seen your parent prune, or cut away, the dead parts. Soon buds appeared in the part of the plant that was left over. With more water and sunlight those buds bloomed, and before long, the plant was alive with new growth again.

The Bible says that Jesus is the vine, and we are the branches. He will work in us so that we can be even bigger blessings in His kingdom. He's also there to take away those things in our lives that stand in the way of our becoming more like Him and bearing more fruit.

There was a man in the Bible who couldn't use his legs. He would sit by a special pool of water that people believed could heal the sick. The man tried to get into the water, only to be moved out of the way by others intent on receiving the gift the water promised. One day the man asked Jesus for help getting into the water, but Jesus' power was greater. He simply told the man to stand—and the man stood up! He told the man to pick up his mat and go on his way. And he did! Jesus pruned away his weakness and healed the man so he could spend the rest of his life producing good fruit!

Jesus, please cut away the distractions that take my eyes off You. Let me live connected to You so I can always be a blessing to others and produce good fruit.

NO PRIDE

God has chosen you. You are holy and loved by Him. Because of this, your new life should be full of loving-pity. You should be kind to others and have no pride. Be gentle and be willing to wait for others.

COLOSSIANS 3:12

There might be some days when you don't feel special, but the truth is you are! The Bible says that God has chosen you! He calls you His precious child and is there to take good care of you all the time. The Bible says you are holy and loved by Him! It might be hard to believe, but all of it is true because God says so.

God says that because of the truths in His Word, your heart should be full of compassion for others. This compassion is like fuel for your world-changing journey as you go about sharing the love of Jesus with those who need to know they matter to Him.

There might be a temptation for people to think that because God is on their side, they can act however they want. But that is the furthest thing from the truth. God goes on to say that His children should not be prideful but instead should seek to put others first. He says the first will be last and the last will be first. As you work on living God's way, don't forget to be kind and patient. You belong to the Lord!

Father God, I can't believe You chose me, but I'm so grateful You did. Teach me how to care about others the way You do. Show me how to have a servant's heart and treat others with compassion just like You do.

YOU ARE SEEN

When Jesus saw their faith, He said to the
sick man, "Son, your sins are forgiven."
MARK 2:5

If you're sad because something didn't go the way you hoped it would, know that your Savior sees you and understands exactly what you're going through. If you're happy because things have been going right, know that Jesus still sees you and is happy for you. He's your biggest cheerleader. In both good times and hard times, He thinks you're something special.

One of the biggest gifts Jesus has given you is the forgiveness of your sins. That alone should give you reason to rejoice—even if you're having a bad day. Remember that you can't do anything holy apart from Jesus. Yes, you can help people and do good things apart from the Lord—but only when you rely on Jesus will your actions make an impact that lasts for eternity.

Jesus wants you to feel secure and confident that He is taking care of you every step of the way. And not only does He forgive you, but because He sees you and knows everything you're dealing with, He is there to provide His peace and comfort and love in unlimited quantities. Let go of all your anxious thoughts and concentrate on Jesus. Rejoice because you are seen by Him—you are wanted and cared for. You can have a great day today because Jesus is on your side!

Lord, sometimes I feel alone. Thank You for Your truth that reminds me
You are watching over me right now. Thank You for looking out for me.

WHO ARE YOU?

Saul answered, "Who are You, Lord?" He said, "I am Jesus, the One Whom you are working against. You hurt yourself by trying to hurt Me."
ACTS 9:5

The man named Saul in today's verse didn't like anyone who believed in Jesus. He was a bitter man filled with anger and rage. His mission in life was to stop people from worshipping the Lord. That is, until he met Jesus.

After a miraculous encounter with Jesus, Saul became known as Paul and devoted the rest of his life to sharing the gospel message of hope and love. He gave his life to change the world so that as many people as possible could come to know Jesus and have their lives transformed for good.

Saul had literally been blinded by a supernatural light. He fell to the ground and heard a voice asking him, "Why are you working so hard against Me?" (Acts 9:4). That's when he asked the Lord who He was. Jesus told him and gave him instructions to go into the city. From that moment on, Saul would be no more. The new creation, the person radically changed by Jesus, was now called Paul.

Who is Jesus to you? If He truly is your everything, don't waste another minute worrying about what today might bring. Live for Him and never forget to tell people who He really is!

Lord, I'm grateful the Bible is filled with all the emotions I experience. The story of Saul's conversion helps me know more of who You are. You are my Savior who lives and who pursues His children. You are the King who has great plans for us and helps us succeed by the power of Your love!

HAVE MERCY

"But go and understand these words, 'I want loving-kindness and not a gift to be given.' For I have not come to call good people. I have come to call those who are sinners."

MATTHEW 9:13

Jesus wants us to be about mercy instead of sacrifice. Rather than giving up, He wants you to give away your compassion as you interact with your friends and family and teachers and other grown-ups. Wherever you are, make sure to share His mercy with a world that so desperately needs His love.

Jesus made it clear that He came to deal with the problem of sin. He said that healthy people don't need a doctor—sick people do. Changing your world requires having the same mindset Jesus has. He didn't isolate Himself. Jesus was all about relationships and preached to the people who did life with Him. He spent time with them so they could see by His actions just how much He loved and cared for them.

Instead of being selfish and making decisions that always put you first, think about ways you can serve other people. When you act like Jesus and make other people feel important, you are changing the world. When you are kind and respectful to others, you are treating them the way Jesus treats them, showing them that they matter. Through your actions, you are showing people what the gospel looks like in real life!

Lord, I really want to treat other people like You would treat them. I want to be Your hands and feet so that I'm sharing the gospel not only with words but also through my actions.

RIGHT LIVING

*But you, man of God, turn away from all these sinful things.
Work at being right with God. Live a God-like life. Have
faith and love. Be willing to wait. Have a kind heart.*

1 TIMOTHY 6:11

Just as sharing your faith with a friend requires courage and hard work, deciding to walk away from doing the wrong thing also requires a lot of courage and hard work. Jesus wants us to be mindful of making good choices. He wants us to know that because He saved us, we no longer live by what the world says. No, as new creations in Christ, we find our way in Him.

Your daily walk with the Lord is so important, because it's your anchor of truth in the storms of everyday life. Things will happen that try to take your mind off doing what's right. All the time thoughts will pop up that cause you to second-guess who you are in Jesus. However, when you see everything that Jesus has done and is doing for you, your faith will grow and you will continue to live life in a way that honors God.

As you follow the Lord Jesus in this life of faith, you can be assured He hears every single one of your prayers. Don't hesitate to tell Him what you need. And keep kindness in your heart so you will continue to treat others well. This is the life of a world changer!

*Jesus, when I think about all the ways You treated people with love and
compassion, I hope that I can do the same. I hope others can see You in me
and that I will have an opportunity to tell them just how amazing You are!*

STAY CONNECTED

My being safe and my honor rest with God. My safe
place is in God, the rock of my strength.
PSALM 62:7

Staying connected to God is the best thing you can do as you go on your world-changing adventure. When you put your life in His hands, you are safe and tied to the source of your ultimate strength. God doesn't see you as a robot, so He will let you decide where you want to go. The best thing you can do is choose to follow where He leads.

Take time today to thank the Lord for all the blessings He's given you. Ask Him for opportunities to share His love with people who cross your path. Don't forget to keep a right attitude. Be respectful to your parents and teachers. Remain connected to God by making good choices and speaking words of truth and love.

See each new day as a gift you get to unwrap, and you will continually discover new ways that God is trying to connect with you. From the sun rising to the birds singing, to the flowers and butterflies and tall trees swaying in the cool breeze. To the moon and stars and your best friends and favorite books and foods and songs. God wants you to know how much you mean to Him. He is your safe place!

Jesus, I can't live this life of faith without You. Help me stay
connected to Your instructions and promises. I don't want to
be selfish. Help me think of others and all the ways I can serve.

WALK IN WISDOM

He who trusts in his own heart is a fool,
but he who walks in wisdom will be kept safe.
PROVERBS 28:26

Making good decisions is super important. It's easy to find ourselves in situations where we make choices based on how we feel. The Bible, however, calls us to be wise—and to make decisions based on the truth of God's Word.

The Bible teaches us to trust God and not our feelings. Mary and Joseph had to do just that. Before Jesus was born, an angel came to Mary and told her she was going to have a baby. This was not an easy thing. Mary was just a teenager, and she was engaged to Joseph. An angel of the Lord came to Joseph too and explained the situation. Joseph prayed and trusted that God was in control. Mary and Joseph got married and took care of baby Jesus. He was their top priority.

As hard as life may be sometimes, stay connected to the Lord by reading His Word and praying. Ask God to give you strength to know the difference between facts and feelings. Use this day the Lord has given you to change the world around you. Go show people how awesome Jesus is!

Lord, it's hard not to react based on feelings.
Feelings change, but Your Word does not. Help me
obey Your truth. Teach me how to be wise.

WITH YOU

*"See, I am with you. I will care for you everywhere you go.
And I will bring you again to this land. For I will not leave
you until I have done all the things I promised you."*

GENESIS 28:15

The enemy would like you to think that each day is just the same old thing and that God is far away. But you know that's not true. God is always with you. He's never far away. Following God means that you stay connected to Him by reading your Bible and listening for His voice. Abraham serves as a good example of someone who stayed connected to God. God had called Abraham to move far away from everything and everyone he knew. And although that seemed scary, God promised to use Abraham in huge ways.

Abraham had great faith. He packed up his family and headed in the direction God told them to go. Remember, this same kind of thing happened to Noah. The ark sailed on the stormy seas for days and days, and when it finally stopped, Noah and his family were far away from the home they had left. But Noah had faith—and it took him and his family exactly where God needed them to be. Do you have a faith this strong, brave boy?

*Jesus, please help me follow Your lead. Help me resist the
temptation to see every day as the same old thing. Instead,
please help me experience each day as a gift from You.
I want to see You in even the smallest of things.*

TURNING

The Lord says, "Cursed is the man who trusts in man, who trusts in the flesh for his strength, and whose heart turns away from the Lord."
JEREMIAH 17:5

Today, think about what is most important in your life. Obviously, your walk with Jesus is at the top of that list. Your parents and family come next. And your world-changing adventure is a key component of your life as well.

Today's Bible verse might seem a little scary, but it really is a positive message about where our priorities should be. Keeping your faith in God and trusting Him for everything you need is a great way to be faithful and obedient to Him. Rely on Him for your strength, and keep your heart connected to His.

When you have your priorities in order, you'll have a much easier time trusting that God is who He says He is and that He will keep His promises. The enemy would like you to put distractions at the top of your list and put God somewhere near the bottom. Keeping God at the top isn't easy when the world tells you so many other things are more important than Him. But all the distractions in life can never fill your heart the way Jesus does. Ask Him to help you keep Him first in your life!

Lord, help me live each day with my priorities in order. Help me put You first in everything I do. Help me walk away from the distractions. Thank You for taking care of me, Jesus.

BIGGER THINGS

*"For sure, I tell you, whoever puts his trust in Me can
do the things I am doing. He will do even greater things
than these because I am going to the Father."*

JOHN 14:12

Jesus wants to reassure you that living for Him allows you to do all the
things He created you to do. And He promises to help you do great things
for His kingdom.

What is it that you feel Jesus is calling you to do? You're not too young
to make a difference. God can do something very special through your obedience. If you haven't started one already, grab a blank notebook and start
a spiritual journal. Write down your thoughts and prayers and quiet-time
reflections. Then later on, look back and see where common themes arise.
Maybe your goal is to become more involved at your church. Or maybe you
can ask your family to volunteer time to help a local food pantry.

Follow the Lord and you will be taken care of. Obey His teachings and
you will be satisfied. Trust Him and you will find yourself doing great things
to bless people and gain favor with the Lord. When you step out in faith,
the Lord will equip you with the resources you need to get the job done.
Be creative and let His light shine.

*Jesus, please help me discover all my talents. I want to do something
special that shows people how much You care about them. Give
me ideas and the courage to follow through. Thank You!*

FOCUSED

How happy is the man who has made the Lord his trust,
and has not turned to the proud or to the followers of lies.
PSALM 40:4

It's important to stay focused on God's plan for you. Reading your Bible will help you learn more and more of the ways God is guiding your heart and life. Trust Him with your life and make a decision today that will affect all your tomorrows. Decide that He is more important than anything. Decide that doing what He says is always the right thing to do.

There's a temptation to listen to people who seem to have all the answers to living a successful life. But the Bible warns us to avoid trusting other people over the one who created us. It's not that God doesn't want us to ask people for advice, but ultimately He wants us to make decisions based on His Word.

God wants you to be confident in who He made you to be. Don't ever feel that you need to change who you are to fit in or to be accepted by people. You are special and God will bring into your life others who also love Him. They will encourage you to read your Bible and grow in your faith. God promises you contentment when you follow Him on your world-changing journey.

Jesus, please help me be confident in who You made me
to be. You don't make mistakes! I want to do what You
say. Guide me on the paths You want me to travel.

THE RIGHT PATH

All the Holy Writings are God-given and are made alive by Him. Man is helped when he is taught God's Word. It shows what is wrong. It changes the way of a man's life. It shows him how to be right with God.
2 TIMOTHY 3:16

The Bible is like a guidebook that shows you how to become more like Jesus. Just as God led the Israelites out of Egypt, He is with you today to take you to the people He wants you to meet and the places He wants you to go.

The Bible isn't just an old book filled with nice sayings. It is living—made alive by God. All the words are from Him and are holy. Not only is the Bible there to show you right from wrong, but it has the power to change your life. It has the power to lead you down the right path and show you how to stay connected with God.

Continue to rely on God for your strength and to walk with Him through each new day He gives you. As you work to change the world, stay on the path of His peace and look for ways to grow even closer to Him. Share the holy name of Jesus with the people you meet along the way.

Jesus, please help me develop a good habit of not only reading Your Word every day but also being eager to do so! I pray that it will encourage me to stay connected to You always.

HAPPY

O Lord of all, how happy is the man who trusts in You!
PSALM 84:12

God wants you to trust Him, because then you can be confident He has you right where you need to be. The Bible promises that you'll be your happiest when you're trusting Him and following His rules.

There are a lot of things in life that make us happy, but the biggest priority in your life should be walking with the Lord. He will make you happy 100 percent of the time! You can trust Him even on the days when it doesn't seem like He hears your prayers. The truth is, He always hears you, but His timeline is different from yours. He is always faithful and will always do the best thing for you. He is the one who defends you and supports you and loves you.

The book of Genesis records a true story about a man named Joseph. His brothers sold him into slavery. The slave traders took him to Egypt and sold him to an important official there. But before long Joseph was sent to prison because of a false accusation against him. He spent a long time behind bars but never lost his faith in God, believing that God loved him despite his circumstances. By the end of the story, Joseph became second-in-command under the pharaoh over all of Egypt. From prison to palace, the one thing that never changed was Joseph's trust in God. Joseph knew where true happiness comes from.

Dear Lord, there are days when I feel down and can't seem to find joy. Please remind me that my happiness will come from knowing that You love me and protect me and guide me all the days of my life.

ENDURING LOVE

Trust in the Lord forever. For the
Lord God is a Rock that lasts forever.
ISAIAH 26:4

The enemy will always try to distract you from your world-changing mission. He will try to get you to second-guess yourself when it comes to the things God is calling you to do. God is your rock, and your life is built on His truth and promises. The storms of the devil's lies can't wash away your faith and hope.

Jesus told His friends a parable about a foolish man building his house on sand and a wise man building his house on rock. When raging floodwaters came, the house on the sand was knocked over and washed away, while the house on the rock stood firm. Being wise means that you trust what you read in your Bible to be true and that you believe Jesus loves you and is on your side.

Make it a daily habit to praise God for all the blessings He gives you. Don't get bogged down in distractions. Don't let life's let-downs get the best of you. Pray for strength to rise above the difficulties, and understand that God is so much bigger than your biggest problem or concern. That's why He spends so much time reminding you not to worry or be afraid—He holds you in the palm of His hand.

Lord, I know You love me, and I'm sorry for all the times I
forget You're in charge. I'm so grateful for You. Please help
me focus on You and not give in to life's distractions.

COMPASSION

How great is Your loving-kindness! You have stored it
up for those who fear You. You show it to those
who trust in You in front of the sons of men.
PSALM 31:19

It's easy to go along with the crowd. Your job as a world changer for Jesus is to stand up for Him even if no one else will. Showing other people that you trust Jesus is a great way to be a witness for Him. He wants to reassure you that nothing you do for Him is ever wasted.

The exciting thing is that God's love for you will never run out. The Bible says He has stored up compassion for you. He's big enough to handle a million prayers and more from you. He's strong enough to love you and carry you through every storm and trial. He smiles when He sees you. Yes, the Lord of the universe thinks you're something special.

Dream up new plans for telling people who Jesus really is, and let His compassion be the fuel that takes you places you never thought you could go on your own. Maybe you'll bake a cake and deliver it to an elderly neighbor. Maybe you'll make cards for people at a local nursing home. Sharing His compassion with others is a great way to be the hands and feet of Jesus.

Lord, please help me think of ways to make a
difference for Your glory. I really want to share
the compassion You have for me with others.

PEACEFUL DAYS

I will lie down and sleep in peace.
O Lord, You alone keep me safe.
PSALM 4:8

Your schedule can be overwhelming sometimes. You might feel like you're trapped in an endless loop of doing homework and keeping up with chores and running errands with your family. But since the Lord promises you peaceful days, you may need to change the way you look at things.

The Lord is protecting you and looking out for you always. So try to see each day as a gift you get to unwrap, as an opportunity to discover something new about Jesus. He loves you and desires to show you more of who He is. He wants to take away your worries and fears.

Today, right in the middle of your day, be intentional about talking to the Lord and thanking Him for the gift of life. Thank Him for your friends and your talents. If you're not sure of your talents, that's a great thing to talk to Him about too. Having the right outlook helps you stay plugged in to the Lord's peace. Changing the world isn't a fast race but rather a marathon of days and weeks and years. During that time, you can be a great influence on the people around you as the peace that Jesus gives you flows out to them. Be confident that you are useful to the Lord!

Father God, I need Your peace in my life. I have to admit there are days
when I feel like my life serves no purpose. But I know better, because
You don't make mistakes and You care about me. Please continue to
teach me how I can change my corner of the world for Your glory.

TRUE

*Every word of God has been proven true. He is
a safe-covering to those who trust in Him.*
PROVERBS 30:5

As you go about your day, find confidence and strength in the fact that God always tells the truth. He loves you. His Word promises that He will never go back on what He tells you, and He will never change His mind. He thought you were super special yesterday, and He thinks the same thing today.

Is there something you've been asking God for, but you feel like He hasn't answered that particular prayer? Do you feel like He's off helping other people and has left you all alone? Are there things that have happened in your life that you just don't understand, and you wish God would give you an explanation? The beautiful thing about God is that He is real and His heart for you is real. That means He has heard each prayer you've prayed and will answer every one of them. He has promised all these things in His Word, and He is the promise keeper.

God will never leave you alone and will never forget you. God has never removed you from His grip, and through all of the good things and all of the hard things He covers you. He feels your pain and sadness, and He celebrates every joy with you. The Lord is the one sure thing in your life, and He wants you to know how much you mean to Him.

*Lord, help me not to live my life by feelings but by every truth that I find
in Your Word. Thank You for hearing me and guiding me and loving me.*

HONESTLY

"God is not a man, that He should lie. He is not a son of man, that He should be sorry for what He has said. Has He said, and will He not do it? Has He spoken, and will He not keep His Word?"

NUMBERS 23:19

There will be times in life when you feel disappointed that things didn't go the way you planned. The good news is that even though things in life change quite often, God never does! You don't have to worry that God will suddenly stop caring about you. If God says He's going to do something, He does it!

The Lord wants you to trust Him. He is in charge, and His plans for you are good. He has called you to go out and change the world by sharing His love with your friends, family, and other people who cross your path. He knows this will fill your heart and bring Him glory.

One of God's best qualities (they're all amazing!) is His honesty. You will find countless examples of it in His Word. He found Adam and Eve in the garden after they had sinned, and He promised to take care of them—and He did! It was the same with Noah. The Lord told Noah to build a big boat, and Noah obeyed. As a result, he and his family were saved from the flood! The Bible contains many more true stories of God saying something and following through. You can't find a single promise He made that He didn't keep!

You matter to Jesus. He's proud of you for following Him. That's the truth!

Lord, I'm grateful I never have to wonder if Your Word is true or false. Thank You for Your love and for the reminder that You will always be honest.

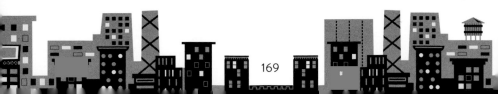

NO SHAME

Wait for the Lord. Be strong. Let your heart be strong. Yes, wait for the Lord.
PSALM 27:14

God doesn't want you to feel shame when you make mistakes. No one is perfect. No matter how hard you try, you're bound to mess up at some point. Don't waste time being afraid that the Lord is upset with you. Instead, if you mess up, ask Him for forgiveness and then move on.

The enemy continually tries to sidetrack you from doing your world-changing job. He wants you to second-guess yourself and wonder if your mistakes might prevent you from being good enough for God's love. But. . .

Jesus gave up His life to save you. He loves you *that* much. He endured all the pain and shame of the cross because He loves you *that* much. Your mistakes can never be big enough to undo what Jesus did for you. Today, connect with your Jesus. Thank Him for everything He has done to rescue you from the world's darkness. Make today about celebrating Him. Let your decisions, words, and actions rise up like a song of praise to Jesus. He is worthy!

Thank You for giving me today, Lord. I'm sorry for all the bad decisions I've made. Please forgive me. Please help me make today all about You and not about me.

MOUNTAIN MOVER

*"For sure, I tell you, a person may say to this mountain,
'Move from here into the sea.' And if he does not doubt,
but believes that what he says will be done, it will happen."*
MARK 11:23

You are stronger than you think! Jesus told His friends that if they would just believe in Him then they would have unimaginable power. That doesn't mean you can go to the gym and bench-press 500 pounds. But it does mean that you have His power and resources at your disposal to share the gospel. If you have faith and believe in the one who is sending you, He will use you to move mountains of hardened hearts—so that people will feel and experience the love Jesus has for them.

If you spend daily prayer time with the Lord, you will find that you are braver and more confident than you previously thought. Ask Jesus to reveal His plans for your life. Ask Him to help you live out your faith in bold new ways.

Changing the world doesn't happen overnight. The apostle Paul went on four world-changing journeys in his life, and for most of those journeys he was in stressful situations. But thousands of years later, people are still learning from his writings—and we get a bigger picture of who Jesus really is from them. Keep working, brave boy! You are stronger than you think!

Jesus, I want my faith to grow. Help me to look in the mirror and see what You see. Help me to become the brave world changer You created me to be. I love You, Lord!

CHANGED!

Let God change your life. First of all, let Him give you a new mind. Then you will know what God wants you to do. And the things you do will be good and pleasing and perfect.

ROMANS 12:2

The people Jesus saves become new creations. His love for them gets rid of their old ways and creates beautiful new ones. If you are saved, you are changed!

The scriptures say that part of this good change is a new mind—a new way of thinking about things. Jesus wants you to see each day as a chance to tell the world about Him. He wants you to read your Bible and give all your life to Him by obeying His rules. Remember, He always wants what's best for you, so having a new way of thinking will help you live out His plans for your life.

The people Jesus called to follow Him had jobs that provided money for them and their families. After they met Jesus, they were changed. They started living their lives literally *for* Him and *with* Him. That's why Jesus said they would begin to fish for men, meaning they would change the world by sharing His message of love one person at a time. Jesus is calling you today, just like He called His disciples. He's calling you to follow Him and share the gospel with the world. Go and share your changed life. When you do, people will get a bigger, better picture of Jesus!

Lord, please continue to change my thoughts. Help me think about Your words. Help me think about the way You treat people so that I can be more like You.

WORLDWIDE

*He said to them, "You are to go to all the world
and preach the Good News to every person."*
Mark 16:15

The Bible is clear that we should be world changers by telling people everywhere about Jesus. You might be thinking that's a goal you will never be able to meet. But the truth of the matter is you can reach more people than you think.

For example, with your parents' permission, you could start your own YouTube channel and use that as a kind of ministry to reach people all over with the gospel message. You could share daily or weekly Bible verses and discuss the things Jesus is teaching you. You could share your favorite songs as a way to point people to God. The possibilities are endless when it comes to reaching people for Jesus. Or if you like to write and express yourself creatively, you could start your own blog. You could post inspirational thoughts and stories of ways you've seen Jesus at work in your life and the lives of others.

Get creative and come up with other ways you could share the gospel message. When you pray and put your mind to it, you'll be amazed at the ideas you will have to take the message of Jesus worldwide!

*Lord, please show me new ways of telling people
about You. Help me reach the people who
need to hear how much You love them.*

READY TO TEACH

If you do not have wisdom, ask God for it. He is always ready to give it to you and will never say you are wrong for asking.

JAMES 1:5

The Lord wants to teach you so many awesome things about who He is and what He has in store for you. He wants to show you things in His Word and help you understand all there is to know about His message of hope. The Bible says He wants you to ask Him for wisdom because He's ready to teach you. And the cool thing is He will never get tired of you asking.

It's like when you're taking a class you don't feel confident about. You might be embarrassed to ask your teacher questions, so you try to figure things out on your own. But that's not what God wants from you. He loves you and wants you to ask Him questions. He wants you to share with Him anything and everything that's on your heart. He wants to talk to you and teach you all the time, because you are so deeply treasured by Him.

As you read your Bible, it's always a good idea to keep a notebook where you can write down ideas and thoughts and feelings and lessons God is teaching you. You can jot down questions you have or verses that are hard to understand and go to the Lord in prayer about them. You'll be amazed at how much you'll start to learn about a lot of different things!

Lord, please teach me Your ways. Show me the lessons I need to learn. Help me stay humble. I always want to have a teachable heart.

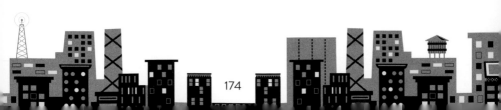

TELL THE NATIONS

"This Good News about the holy nation of God must be preached over all the earth. It must be told to all nations and then the end will come."

MATTHEW 24:14

Today's verse is like the mission statement for your world-changing journey. Jesus told His friends that His gospel of good news had to be preached throughout the whole world, among every nation, before He returns. When you think about being a part of this great adventure, think about all the ways you can make a difference.

Maybe you like to draw. You could create cool pictures of different events in the Bible. Then you could write Bible verses to go with your pictures to make them complete. You could take a picture of your work and ask your parents to post it on social media. That's a great way to send out the gospel message to a wider audience.

Maybe you like to bake or make things. Perhaps you could consider starting a small business baking cookies or making crafts and then using the money you earn to support a charity. Always remember that you're never too young to inspire others. And who knows, somebody who sees you using your talents for Jesus might be inspired to use theirs too. That's a great way to keep growing and spreading the love of God to the world.

Jesus, please help me figure out ways I can use the gifts You've given me to bless others. Help me think bigger than my own little corner of the world.

THE SENDING

Then Jesus said to them again, "May you have peace. As the Father has sent Me, I also am sending you."
JOHN 20:21

It's important not to waste the life you've been given. Jesus says that He wants His children to have peace, and He also wants them to move and act for His kingdom's purposes. Jesus wants you to share His peace with people everywhere!

Jesus had relationships with people. He let them know they mattered and that they were loved. The people who understood Jesus was the Messiah always wanted to be around Him. He made sure that people who were hurting found healing. People who felt alone found company. People who felt unwanted found love.

You can treat people the same way Jesus treated them. He showed respect to those who came to Him for help and gave them His peace. As you let Jesus send you to different people and places, consider ways you can be His hands and feet. Consider ways of talking to people to make them want to know more about Jesus. You can do amazing things for the Lord. So don't waste time—dream big and go for it!

I want to be like the apostle Paul and tell everyone I meet about You, Jesus. Help me connect my talents to Your gospel so I can be really effective on my world-changing journey.

GOD RULES!

How beautiful on the mountains are the feet of him who brings good news, who tells of peace and brings good news of happiness, who tells of saving power, and says to Zion, "Your God rules!"
ISAIAH 52:7

God loves for His good news to be shared with people who are looking for answers. The good news of what Jesus did for the world is a beautiful message of hope and love.

Peace is another thing God commands us to spread. You've heard the Golden Rule about treating others the way you want them to treat you— it's kind of the same thing with the Lord's peace. Giving it away to all the people you meet is the way to change your world one heart at a time. And then peace will make its way back to fill your heart over and over again.

The joy of the Lord and His saving power are two more things God loves for you to share with others. As you tell people about the saving power of Jesus, you are planting the seeds of joy in their lives. When your conversations contain these messages, people will want to know more about the Lord and His goodness. That's when you can testify to the fact that your God rules!

Lord, please show me the way to spread Your peace and love to the world. Show me how to be bold and proclaim Your majesty to the nations.

IN HIS NAME

"It must be preached that men must be sorry for their sins and turn from them. Then they will be forgiven. This must be preached in His name to all nations beginning in Jerusalem."
Luke 24:47

You've come a long way on your world-changing journey, and you should be proud of all you've done to make Jesus famous. Remember that each day is a gift you've been given to continue the path that leads you to new places and new people.

Your life is the message of hope people will see. Then they will begin to ask questions. You are learning so much through your daily Bible reading. You are doing a great job letting Jesus teach you in your quiet times with Him. Those are the lessons you can share when people ask you questions about what Jesus has done. As far as your influence reaches, so will the world be changed for God's glory. Tell others that accepting Jesus as their Savior and turning from their sins is the only answer they need for all of life's questions.

The name of Jesus is powerful. In His name, people are saved from sin and despair. In His name, hope is found and lives are restored. In the name of Jesus, the name above all names, stay strong and continue to preach the gospel message!

Thank You, Jesus, for letting me be a part of sharing Your gospel with the world. Thank You for sending me to tell people how much You love them and how much they matter!

ALL FOR THE LORD

Whatever work you do, do it with all your heart.
Do it for the Lord and not for men.
COLOSSIANS 3:23

Sometimes you can take shortcuts to get where you're going. If you've seen your parents use a GPS app, you know it helps them avoid traffic so they can get to where they're going quicker. But when it comes to doing your schoolwork and chores and changing the world, there are zero shortcuts. Whether you're doing your math homework or helping your parents with yard work, you need to do all of it like you're working for Jesus.

Doing something with all your heart means you care about giving it your best—because that's what Jesus gave for you. He didn't just come to earth and do half the job of saving you. He went all the way to the cross and gave up His life so you could find yours. He defeated death so that you could too!

When you do everything like you're doing it for the Lord, people will see a difference in you. They'll wonder why you have a great attitude no matter what it is you're doing. And that's the open door you'll be able to walk through to share the name of Jesus. When they ask for the reason you're so happy, whether you're mowing the yard, taking out the trash, or doing your homework, you will be able to tell them Jesus is the reason!

Lord, I'm sorry for complaining so much about all the things
I have to do. Thank You for the reminder that my life shows
gratitude when I work like I'm working only for You!

HIS GREATNESS

"Tell of His greatness among the nations.
Tell of His great works among all the people."
1 Chronicles 16:24

When you think of all the ways you can share how great God is, remember you can use more than your words. Your actions are another powerful way to show people how awesome He is!

The book of Psalms in your Bible is a great example of the way people used words to try to express the greatness of God. A lot of the psalms were written by King David, who had a close relationship with the Lord. He spent a lot of time trying to capture just how amazing God was to him. David told how God was his safe place and his strength. He told of God's unfailing love and of all the ways the Lord had been his provider and rescuer.

It's impossible for us humans to accurately express God's greatness to the world. Your job is just to try. Through words and actions, paint the greatest picture of God you can. God wants to use you to show the world that there is real hope in Him. Show others His goodness. Tell of His great deeds. Let people know what He means to you and what He can do for them.

Lord, I want to be bold and brave and confident enough to tell the
world about Your awesome greatness. I pray that my words and actions
can paint at least a small picture of just how mighty You are.

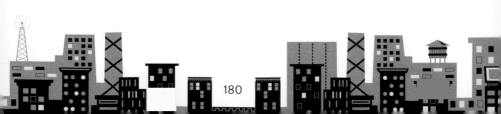

THE GIVER OF GIFTS

*God has given each of you a gift. Use it to help
each other. This will show God's loving-favor.*
1 PETER 4:10

God has blessed you with a unique combination of special abilities. Out of everyone God created, He only made one you. He wants you to use your special qualities to be a blessing to others. He wants you to use your skills to share His compassion with others. When you use your uniqueness for God, you show others just how amazing He is.

Maybe you're not sure what gifts and talents God has given you. Just ask the Lord to help you see them. Some people are good at listening and making other people feel wanted. Some people are highly creative and like to make cards or art or poems for other people. Some are good at giving their time to help other people know they matter. Once you discover your talents, be brave and use them to show people how much God loves them.

The people you read about in your Bible did this exact thing. They used the gifts God gave them to spread the love of Jesus to the world. God is calling you right now to use your gifts. Believe in yourself, because He does! Spend some time today coming up with a plan to be a gift giver just like God is.

*Lord, I know You have given me talents to use as a blessing
to others. Please help me use those talents to show people
just how loving and compassionate You are.*

FEET OF BEAUTY

And how can someone tell them if he is not sent? The Holy Writings say, "The feet of those who bring the Good News are beautiful."
ROMANS 10:15

Being a part of God's kingdom plan is a beautiful thing. You have a very special calling, because the one who made you is sending you out into the world to be a representative of His grace and truth.

Going outside your comfort zone is a way to reach more people with the good news of Jesus. For example, you might be on a sports team or part of an after-school group where a lot of different kids get together. These are great places to talk about Jesus. It doesn't have to be awkward. In the natural flow of conversation, you could say things like, "The Lord has blessed me so much." Or, "Jesus really helps me." Or, "Without the Lord, I don't have any good thing."

You might be able to go on mission trips as you get older. Those are fantastic, but just going to school or practice is also living on mission. God is overjoyed when you obey His command to share Jesus with everyone you meet. Remember, though, that there's a difference between talking down to people and talking *to* them. The people who talk down are not effective, but the people who talk *to* others are communicating with love and kindness and respect. Those are the conversations the Lord calls beautiful.

Lord, I really am thankful I have a chance to practice sharing Your truth and love with my friends. Please open doors for me to be able to talk to people about how great You are and how much You love them.

TEACH AND PRAY

*"Then we will use all of our time to
pray and to teach the Word of God."*
ACTS 6:4

When Jesus was young, His parents found Him teaching in a local synagogue. He was reading from the book of Isaiah. Specifically, He was reading from chapter 61, which says He came to help the brokenhearted heal and to share the good news of salvation. Jesus taught as He read from the prophet's words that He came to set the captives free and release the prisoners from darkness. Can you imagine being there listening to the Savior of the world read from the sacred book?

Now is a good time for you to go find the book of Isaiah in your Bible and read chapter 61. Pray that God would move in your heart and teach you what He wants you to do. Jesus said He came to bring comfort to those who are mourning and to put a crown of beauty on their head instead of ashes. You can be like Jesus in your world. You have the power to be a light and to spread joy where there's sadness, and praise where there's despair!

All the wonderful things Jesus mentioned in the synagogue that day are the same things He's doing in your heart. Let Him continue to be the Lord of your life, and follow Him wherever He leads you. Keep praying. And when you have the opportunity, teach people about His wonderful love.

*Lord, please help me take the message of Isaiah 61 into my
community so that people who are hurting and in desperate
need of You might finally find peace in Your holy name.*

GO AND GATHER

"Do you not say, 'It is four months yet until the time to gather grain'? Listen! I say to you, open your eyes and look at the fields. They are white now and waiting for the grain to be gathered in."

John 4:35

Don't wait. Start planning more ways you can be a part of the harvest. Jesus was telling His friends they didn't need to wait around until they felt good enough or smart enough to tell people about Him. He was saying that wherever they looked, there would be people who needed salvation.

To take it a step further, notice how Jesus mentions the people are not only ready but *waiting* to hear the good news. He's saying their hearts are tender and ready to receive His love. Remember that Jesus is the one who saves, so you don't have to worry about saying everything just right or having enough Bible knowledge. God has your back!

Think about the wind. It blows because that's what it does. If you're lucky enough to be sitting outside on a beautiful spring day, you'll feel the peaceful breeze blow over you. It rustles the leaves as it goes on its journey. It doesn't stop to think about whether it's doing a good job—it just keeps blowing. Be the spiritual wind that takes the good news of Jesus to many souls, bringing them relief as you go.

I'm so thankful You brought me comfort and salvation, Lord. I'm grateful You love me and want me to be a part of the harvest of souls for Your kingdom. Thank You for calling me to share Your name across the world.

SAVING THE LOST

"For the Son of Man came to look for and to save from the punishment of sin those who are lost."
LUKE 19:10

Jesus left His throne and came to earth to save lost souls. He came to heal the brokenhearted and bring light to the people living in darkness. He came to offer His love to hurting hearts. Jesus has a mission of hope and salvation.

As you continue your world-changing journey, keep in mind there are people who don't know Jesus. You may be the first person they listen to when you tell them about the Lord and His wonderful plan of salvation. You may be the first brave disciple to tell them Jesus died, was buried, and rose again to give them hope. You may be the first person who enables them to feel the love of Christ flowing from your words and actions into their soul. They may ask Jesus to become their Lord and Savior all because you were brave enough to want to change the world!

Jesus reminds us that He's the Good Shepherd and we're His sheep. Even if just one is lost, He leaves the flock and goes to rescue the one that needs rescuing. Look and listen for people in your world who need help. God is proud of you for sharing the name of Jesus!

Lord, I'm so grateful You saved me. Soften my heart so I can always be on the lookout for people who are in desperate need of You. Thank You for letting me be a part of this wonderful journey.

EVERLASTING LOVE

*"For God so loved the world that He gave His only Son.
Whoever puts his trust in God's Son will not be
lost but will have life that lasts forever."*

JOHN 3:16

What a journey! You are making plans and sharing the good news of Jesus. What an exciting time in your life when you can know, without a doubt, that you are making a difference in the world as you make Jesus famous. It's so awesome to know that you are a brave young man who is on fire for the Lord!

Today's verse is very popular and often quoted, as it should be. It seems to be the epic summary of the entire Bible. It's the motto of Christians everywhere to share Jesus with the world. God loves everyone so much, and He is saddened to see all the hurting souls in this world. He loved us so much that He decided to send His only Son, Jesus, down into our dark world as a light of eternal hope. He sent Jesus to us so that whoever would put their trust in Him would find a life that lasts forever.

Keep trusting Jesus. He is transforming your life in amazing ways. Stay connected to His Word. Pray boldly. Expect Him to use you to do *big* kingdom work! Be faithful in everything you do, and always seek new ways to make Him famous.

*Jesus, I trust You. You are my King. Please keep using me to share
the good news. I want to change the world for Your glory!*

SCRIPTURE INDEX

OLD TESTAMENT

MORE ENCOURAGEMENT AND WISDOM FOR BRAVE BOYS LIKE YOU!

100 Adventurous Stories for Brave Boys

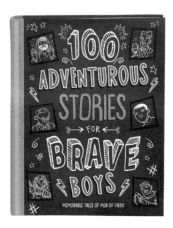

Boys are history-makers! And this deeply compelling storybook proves it! This collection of 100 adventurous stories of Christian men—from the Bible, history, and today—will empower you to know and understand how men of great character have made an impact in the world and how much smaller our faith (and the biblical record) would be without them.

Hardback / 978-1-64352-356-9